PRAISE FOR CHARLIE GARBUTT

A True Southern Gentleman: Any reference book which should include such a definition could simply use Charlie Garbutt as the description of a true southern gentleman.

From our very first phone conversation when looking for a partner on the Old Governor's Mansion, Charlie's response was one of soft-spoken simplicity: "Why do you need me?" As a contractor, there could be many responses. We talked, and the pride in his father's work ethic serving the community with a drug store, his personal commitment to the industry by leading AGC, and sincere caring for his long-time staff at Garbutt Construction were immediately noticed as being part of what makes Charlie unique. He comes up with creative ways to sell an owner on why his team is best qualified to be of service with a straightforward "The stars are in perfect alignment," which, when combined with his honest persona, can close the deal and quickly win a project. But it's not enough to simply sell. Charlie knows and manages the details of each of his projects. He has ownership with the personal delivery of the "Close Out Express" red wagon at the end of each project. When Charlie calls you a friend, you know it truly means something. I am reminded every Christmas with the treasured "secret family recipe" jar I receive.

So, Charlie, to answer your question to your original statement from so many years ago, "Why do you need me?" It is simple. Our world needs more folks like you, Charlie Garbutt. Our lives are made of memories, and working with and knowing Charlie Garbutt is one of those memories, both personally and professionally, I will never forget.

—Ronald Staley, FAPT

Senior Vice President, The Christman Company

Charlie Garbutt is a well-recognized and respected leader in our industry. I have known Charlie for almost twenty years through our work together at the Associated General Contractors organization, as well as from partnering on projects. Charlie is known and has always been recognized for his skill, integrity, and responsibility within the construction industry. I am honored to call Charlie Garbutt a mentor, partner, and friend. Charlie is also recognized within the industry as a leader in Lean Construction implementation and training.

—Doug Davidson
Chairman/CEO, New South Construction

Georgia Military College has participated as the using agency in two recent projects with Garbutt Construction, utilizing Lean Construction Planning. Lean planning proved to be critical in meeting the schedule on both projects. The first project was the renovation of a one-hundred-plus-year-old vacant structure, and the second was a green field project. Lean planning allowed the superintendent and the subcontractors to readily see conflicts before they occurred and develop alternative plans to avoid them. Critical requirements for the system to function properly are accurate information from the subs and a knowledgeable superintendent to manage the process. I am absolutely certain that Lean planning smoothed the construction process, resulting in lower cost and improved delivery for Georgia Military College.

—Jeff Gray
Vice President of Engineering, Georgia Military College

Charlie Garbutt often refers to his "small construction company," but Charlie is no small contractor. Just the opposite, in fact. He looms large as a leader, learner, and liver-by-example. Gandhi said: "There go my people. I must follow them, for I am their leader." Charlie's "people" are his colleagues, subcontractors, and suppliers who assemble to also make challenging "pilgrimages." How he engages them in the service of building and restoring structures is the essential lesson of this important and valuable story.

—Tony Aeck, FAIA

Lord Aeck Sargent

Meet a true Lean champion. Charlie is a creative thinker and a leader in his market. For years, he has successfully focused on ways to set his company apart from the competition and deliver value to his customers. Early on, Charlie embraced the concepts of Lean Construction and incorporated them into his organization. Read Charlie's story and be inspired to improve your organization.

—James Braswell

CM-Lean, LEED-AP, President, Langston Construction Company

LEAN

CONSTRUCTION

CONSTRUCTION

A SMALL CONTRACTOR'S JOURNEY

CHARLIE GARBUTT

Published by Advantage, Charleston, South Carolina.
Member of Advantage Media Group.

ADVANTAGE is a registered trademark, and the Advantage colophon is a trademark of Advantage Media Group, Inc.

Printed in the United States of America.

10 9 8 7 6 5 4 3 2 1

ISBN: 978-1-59932-835-5
LCCN: 2017946899

Cover design by Katie Biondo.
Layout design by Megan Elger.

This publication is designed to provide accurate and authoritative information in regard to the subject matter covered. It is sold with the understanding that the publisher is not engaged in rendering legal, accounting, or other professional services. If legal advice or other expert assistance is required, the services of a competent professional person should be sought.

Advantage Media Group is proud to be a part of the Tree Neutral® program. Tree Neutral offsets the number of trees consumed in the production and printing of this book by taking proactive steps such as planting trees in direct proportion to the number of trees used to print books. To learn more about Tree Neutral, please visit **www.treeneutral.com**.

Advantage Media Group is a publisher of business, self-improvement, and professional development books. We help entrepreneurs, business leaders, and professionals share their Stories, Passion, and Knowledge to help others Learn & Grow. Do you have a manuscript or book idea that you would like us to consider for publishing? Please visit **advantagefamily.com** or call **1.866.775.1696**.

In memory of my father, Robert "Rusty" Garbutt,
who taught me the nobility of hard work

TABLE OF CONTENTS

FOREWORD

Twenty years ago, in 1997, the two founders of Lean Construction in America (and eventually the entire world), Glenn Ballard and Greg Howell, came to see Leo Linbeck, the president of the construction company where I worked, and me to tell us about what they were founding—a new way to see.

They had learned about the Toyota Production System and believed that its philosophy, principles, and concepts, and a very big concept of their own, could revolutionize and greatly improve design and construction. It has.

They were calling it Lean Construction, after the term that three MIT professors had used to describe what Toyota had been doing: Lean Manufacturing.

Lean Manufacturing and Lean Construction have been revolutionizing the world.

Our company and four others put forth funds for Ballard and Howell to found the Lean Construction Institute. Those of us there at the beginning, and our projects, became laboratory settings for experimenting with, learning about, and improving Lean Construction.

What Glenn Ballard and Greg Howell were teaching us, and leading us to try, was very different from "the way we had always done" construction.

While many of us were intrigued by, and trying, these fresh new ideas and their results, change is hard for people. There were doubters, and regular refrains from those were, "We already do all of that stuff, have been for years. We just call it something else," or, "I've been doing construction for thirty years, and I see no reason to change," or, "This will just turn out to be the flavor of the month, and no one will be paying any attention to this in a couple of years."

Twenty years later, not only are people still learning and applying Lean Construction, but it has spread all over the world and is approaching, if not already at, the tipping point for the way facilities will be designed and constructed for the foreseeable future . . . .

I was lucky, twenty years ago, because life events and my response to them had recently opened me up to welcome change and to see where it might take me. I found that to be so much more intriguing than just doing things the same old way.

A little over twenty-one years ago, I was presented with some major opportunities to begin to reinvent myself and the way I saw things. It is important to say "begin to reinvent myself," because such a task can never be completed in a lifetime, but beginning, continuing, and unlocking fresh new ideas is an exciting way to live.

Changes in my personal life showed me the possibility to become unstuck from whom I might have been, forever. I bought a forty-year-old Volkswagen oval window sedan (sixty years old now) as my only car. Sensing a potential new view of my world, I named my Volkswagen "Paradigm Shift."

I began to look and listen in a new and better way.

Paradigm Shift, (PS, for short) was the first guide along this new pathway. The second guide became my spiritual muse, Nancy, who opened my heart to new voices, new rooms. Leo set us upon our Lean Journey. A fourth was David Neenan, a teacher, architect, and builder, who met conundrums with a fresh new surrender in which he would say, "I don't know nothing yet, but I can learn! If I approach the world as if I already know, how can I learn anything new?"

In turn, David introduced me to the wisdom of Eric Hoffer, who said:

"In times of change, learners inherit the earth; while the (knowers) find themselves beautifully equipped to deal with a world that no longer exists."

Grace Hopper then called to my attention:

"The most dangerous phrase in the language is: 'We've always done it this way.'"

Buckminster Fuller told us that "humans are allergic to and resist change," and, "you never change things by fighting the existing reality. To change something, build a new model that makes the existing model obsolete."

"You cannot change how someone thinks, but you can give them a tool to use which will lead them to think differently."

Building a new model is what my teachers/guides, Glenn Ballard and Greg Howell, did when they developed The Last Planner® System and created the Lean Construction Institute as a research body for studying and improving their new models.

Buckminster Fuller also said:

"If I ran a school, I'd give the average grade to the ones who gave me all the right answers, for being good parrots. I'd give the top grades to those who made a lot of mistakes and told me about them, and then told me what they learned from them."

David Neenan put a large gong in the lobby of his office and made it a part of their culture that when anyone made a mistake, they were expected to ring the gong, inviting others to come and learn from the mistake. At first the gong rang often, but gradually it rang less and less as they learned from their, and others', mistakes. Rather than hide them, they celebrated their mistakes, and learned.

So, for me and my reinvention adventure, I owe many thanks to many, especially Paradigm Shift, Nancy Bolton, Leo Linbeck, Glenn Ballard, Greg Howell, David Neenan, Eric Hoffer, Grace Hopper, Buckminster Fuller, and many other Lean Design and Construction thinkers, teachers, and practitioners.

A great adventure is to reinvent ourselves and continuously learn and improve. Many never give themselves the chance to take such a trip. I am very grateful for my leap.

From these influencers and a freedom of thought arising within me, I discovered Lean Construction. It has been, so far, a twenty-one-year progress of discovery and reinvention. It has become a worldwide revolution from a world of adversary to one of respect, collaboration, trust, better results for all, and a much more satisfactory way to live and work.

Charlie Garbutt has been an adventurer on the road of experimentation, learning, improving, teaching others, and leading the way.

I am keenly interested, along with Charlie and others, in introducing the possibilities of Lean Construction to those who have not heard of it nor have wanted to consider it. Charlie Garbutt's story will give the reader an opportunity to see how well it has affected his projects, clients, designers, specialty trade partners, and suppliers.

Garbutt Construction is primarily employing—with considerable success for its clients, designers, specialty contractors, and suppliers—The Last Planner System of the Lean Construction Institute and other essential Lean Principles. The following are areas in which the participants benefit from using The Last Planner System:

- Improved safety and risk management

- Lean gives us bad news early, so we have more time to overcome it

- Lean projects are proactive rather than reactive

- Higher quality

- Earlier delivery of projects

- Reduced waste

- Increased workflow efficiency

- Increased value to the end user

- Reduced cost

- Increased profitability for all participants

- Brings about greater satisfaction with the project, by all

The gains are the result of many things, but significantly because of:

- Respect for all individuals

- Continuous learning and improvement

- Collaboration, real collaboration

- Always improving relationships

- Optimizing the project and not the piece

Charlie Garbutt, the author of this book, *Lean Construction: A Small Contractor's Journey*, has always been one to experiment, learn, and improve himself, his staff, and the outcomes and values for clients, architects, engineers, specialty trade contractors, and suppliers.

In his absorbing story, Charlie Garbutt tells us how he has developed his company by recognizing and maintaining their essential values: natural and inherent honesty; integrity; respect for the individual; and a deep-seated belief in the Golden Rule.

Like the sculptor who discovers a figure hidden within a block of stone, it's almost as if Charlie Garbutt had been preparing his company for Lean Construction to come along and find Garbutt Construction ready to put it to work.

Read his book and ask him to tell you more about the Garbutt Lean journey, its fruits, and its promising future.

Ed Beck
Lean collaborative builder, teacher, and coach

ABOUT THE AUTHOR

As CEO of Garbutt Construction Company, founded in 1976, Charlie Garbutt oversees the strategic direction and growth of the firm. He is responsible for company operations at the executive level where the firm serves as construction manager, general contractor, and design-builder throughout the state of Georgia. Garbutt Construction has earned a position of high regard as evidenced by its diverse portfolio of projects. Charlie is an emeritus member of the board of regents of the University System of Georgia Facility Advisory Board, emeritus board member for Georgia Southern University's Construction Management Industry Advisory council, and past president of the Associated General Contractors of Georgia group and the Dublin Rotary Club. In addition to his bachelor's degree in building construction management from Auburn University, he is LEED AP certified and certified constructor by the American Institute of Constructors. Charlie currently serves on AGC Georgia's board of directors and is recognized state-wide for his vision and commitment to the industry.

In 2014, Charlie became one of Georgia's first Lean Construction Education Professionals, a designation earned at the AGC national level. Charlie devotes much of his time to teaching staff at Garbutt Construction Company and industry colleagues the advantages of a "leaner" construction industry.

INTRODUCTION

Construction has among the highest, if not *the* highest, failure rates of any business sector[1]—so to do it successfully, you've got to be doing something right.

Construction has always been difficult—since the beginning, the industry has struggled with planning and organizing the activity of *building something.* Managing the process requires the talent of herding cats: various and sundry partners and laborers are brought on board, and making the process work requires getting them all on board, on the same page, and moving in the same direction, even though they all have different agendas and different capabilities.

Check out page 115 at the back of the book for more on Lean Construction.

This book is the story of my journey as a contractor who has been working with these difficulties for quite a while, with a good deal of success. My company, Garbutt Construction, has been in business since 1976. In that time, we have known struggle and success, and we have

---

1   Lou Hirsh, "Businesses That Have High Failure Rates," *Chron,* http://smallbusiness. chron.com/businesses-high-failure-rates-61640.html

1

developed a strategy for constantly raising the bar in everything we do, all aspects of the business, and its growth.

Along the way, we discovered a process and a system that helps us to herd the cats of construction—to get everybody focused in the same direction, with the same agenda, in the same rhythm, and thinking holistically about the project they're working on. Lean Construction does this better than anything else I've ever come across in my forty-two years in the industry. I experimented with Lean, and I found out it's not a bunch of fluff—it really works.

Typically, what happens in construction is a general contractor or builder will come up with a plan. It might be as sophisticated as what we call a Critical Path Method (CPM) schedule; it might not. Then, to make it work, he tries to sell it to as many as thirty or forty subcontractors on the project. Lean's approach is to bring those thirty or forty subcontractors to the table and ask them how *they* can make that work and then try to bring all of that together, collaborate on the best plan, and then hold everyone accountable to it. It's a totally different culture, a totally different mind-set, and it's very effective.

I know this well: Lean is the culmination of a long career in construction, as well as a long educative process that started even before I built my own company from scratch.

STARTING OUT

When I was growing up, my father taught me to work. First, when I was about eight years old, he took me down to the bank, and I took out a loan for sixty-three dollars to buy a power lawnmower. I earned money in the summertime by cutting grass, which had great appeal to me because, when you cut grass, you can see that you're accomplishing something. You work, and you can see the fruits of your labor as you go along. When you're finished, you can turn around and look at that project that you've just completed, which is very satisfying.

Construction is the same way, but on a much larger scale: You can take something that's just an idea, or a dream, or a design, and you make it *real*. You can build a building where there was none, or you can bring a building back to life that had outlived its usefulness, and that's very rewarding. When you are finished, you have a very concrete product that you can turn around and take in.

So, my father taught me not only about hard work but also about the value of having a tangible result of your work and of being able to appreciate the completion of a job well done.

This carried over into my work in construction. When I first started college, I was studying architecture. I was always fascinated by design and liked to play with it. But my father thought that if I were going to design buildings, then I needed to know what it was like to build one. So, after my freshman year in college, I worked a summer job for a local construction company in my hometown of Dublin, Georgia. After that, every summer and every Christmas holiday period I worked construction, and I enjoyed it. Soon enough, I came to the conclusion that my calling was more in the building trade than in the design trade, and so I changed my college major to building construction.

It turned out I was not so much one for sitting in one seat, at a desk, just playing with design or crunching numbers. I like to get out and work, get my hands dirty, and then be able to take a step back and see what I've done at the end of the day. After getting my degree from Auburn University in Alabama, I went to work—first for a general contractor in Auburn, and then back in Dublin, where I started my own business from scratch in 1976.

I have stayed in Dublin ever since. Born, raised, and educated in the Southeast, and having maintained a construction business there for forty years, I know the region's construction market well and have worked all along to keep my company, Garbutt Construction, at the forefront of producing high-quality construction work in this area.

MY COMPANY'S JOURNEY

There has been a great deal of change over the course of the forty-plus years that Garbutt Construction has been in business. It has been a period not only of growth but also of education, for both me personally and for the company as a whole.

Lean Construction: A Small Contractor's Journey shares some of the milestones, obstacles, partnerships, and successes that have gotten us where we are, but the overall story is about what I think of as our "Lean journey": the evolution of the company's culture toward, and eventual adoption of, Lean construction. Lean has been the most significant development in our culture and methods, and plays a central role in our striving to achieve quality and to stay true to our core values.

This is not to say that discovering Lean totally changed the way Garbutt Construction had been doing things over the years. We had actually been moving in the direction of Lean culture all along, on our own initiative, so when I came across Lean, it was like a lightbulb finally came on that made everything I had been thinking about and building the company around come together.

That Lean "lightbulb" moment was the culmination of what had been a forty-year maturing process.

For example, it used to be that a general contractor would do a schedule and maybe stick it up on the wall of the construction trailer, but it was so complicated that only the person who made it could read it—the people who actually did the work couldn't. It also didn't get updated much, so after the schedule of real work changed, which it almost continuously does, that schedule on the wall was obsolete.

So, we said, "You know what? We'd better update these things pretty frequently," and we started updating it monthly, then weekly, refining the scheduling process along the way.

But still the schedule was always sort of dictated, as in: "This is *my* plan of how things are going to happen," and we would see that that didn't always work because maybe what *I* thought could happen wasn't what somebody else, like a subcontractor, thought could happen; or that subcontractor may not have had the resources to make it happen.

Ultimately, Lean is what really brought Garbutt Construction into focus and really made our work a collaborative process. When we have a collaborative process with the subcontractors, we can really put the pedal to the metal on a construction job because everybody is bought in and has committed to the schedule. And scheduling is just one example of the role that Lean played in our maturing.

WHAT IS LEAN CONSTRUCTION?

Today, construction management services, as an industry, is still catching up to these collaboration, scheduling, and process management developments, and there are still lessons to learn.

One of the purposes of this book is to lay out and tell the story of the innovations we have implemented. By sharing our story with you, we hope that you and others involved in the market for construction, from subcontractors to buyers, understand some of the basics of Lean Construction and realize that, if profitability and productivity are concerns for everyone (which they surely are), then it is to everyone's advantage to work with a general contractor that is committed to the culture and quality of Lean.

In the pages ahead, I'll get into more detail about the many ways Garbutt Construction has benefitted from Lean construction principles. But what does "Lean" mean? There are a lot of definitions out there, but from my perspective, the core elements of Lean can be summed up as follows: Lean is a *culture of collaboration, hands-on planning and scheduling, and continuous improvement* that a company adopts to *eliminate waste and increase productivity and quality*. This sums up the key aspects of Lean as Garbutt Construction practices it and as we will discuss in this book.

After discussing the ways that the construction industry has changed in chapter 1, I go on to tell the story of our Lean journey in chapters 2 and 3. This culminates in the implementation of Lean, but involves many other aspects of our evolution, as well.

While our discovery and deployment of Lean is relatively recent, the concepts themselves have had a long journey, as well. They are rooted in the ideas of the engineer W. Edwards Deming, who consulted with Japanese companies after World War II as they rebuilt their economy. These ideas ultimately influenced the Toyota production system, which was very successful in eliminating waste in manufacturing and is considered the original Lean production system. This production system allows manufacturers to produce quality products quickly and economically.

Construction, however, is very different from manufacturing. Builders do not repeatedly produce the same single product over and over but instead work on individual *projects*, each one unique. Because of this, and because construction involves different players on every project, many people assumed that Lean did not apply to construction. As you will see, we've found definitively that Lean has a strong place in the construction industry.

In the remaining chapters of the book, I apply Lean concepts concerning the elimination of waste (chapter 4), project planning (chapter 5), collaboration (chapter 6), and continuous improvement (chapter 7) to the construction sector, using Garbutt Construction's own projects as examples.

Along the way, you will also hear from some key members of my team (my superintendent, Tracy Lively; my project manager, Chris Davis; the current president of the company, Sean Moxley; and my daughter and our head of marketing, J. Charlie Garbutt) about how they view the role of Lean in the journey of Garbutt Construction.

I have found that, like a lot of cultural innovations, Lean Construction has been moving west to east across the country; California has been on the cutting edge, and now others are starting to catch up. The Lean Construction Institute (LCI) has been around since 1997, but many contractors, especially in my region, the Southeast, have been unaware of it until very recently. Over the course of the last several years, Garbutt Construction has developed into a rare specimen in the Southeast: a mid-sized construction firm that has not only adopted but also become an expert in Lean culture and methods. I am confident that we are on the cutting edge or frontier of a major innovative cultural movement in our industry.

Not that we have reached the top of the mountain. A major part of Lean is not only being aware of the state you're in but also never being satisfied with where you are. We are always raising the bar for ourselves, trying to do a better job and improve on all fronts. Every one of our project managers and superintendents is educated in Lean principles and culture. As a result, we are uniquely qualified, especially in our region and market, to continue to provide high quality and high productivity in construction, and to keep improving.

It turns out, what we were doing right all along is what Lean helps us to do better.

But that's not the beginning of the story—we were in business for more than thirty years before discovering Lean, so we must have been doing *something* right. It turns out, what we were doing right all along is what Lean helps us to do *better*. This book tells the story of my, and my company's, journey toward that Lean lightbulb moment and explains how our adoption of Lean allows us to be at the forefront of high-quality construction service in our region.

THE STATE OF CONSTRUCTION
AND COMPANY CULTURE

When I started out in construction in 1976, I had to do things like sit outside all night in the freezing cold (twelve degrees!) with a couple of concrete finishers, the three of us manning a bunch of salamander heaters blowing across the surface of a freshly poured concrete slab to keep it from freezing over. I was certainly not happy about it at the time, but I had to do it to get the job done and to get it done right.

The journey from that point to now has been a long one, during which I have a taken on continuously bigger and more complex projects, developed the expertise of the company in the areas of historical restoration and adaptive reuse, and had major successes, such as the restoration of the Old Governor's Mansion on the campus of Georgia College in Milledgeville. I adopted Lean along the way and first had a major success with that in working on the Old

First National Bank building in downtown Dublin, Georgia, my hometown.

I still maintain the commitment to quality work that, forty-some years ago, made me sit all night in the freezing cold; and while I'm proud of my successes, I may be even prouder of a time when I almost *didn't* succeed—namely, the early 1990s, when the construction economy tanked. I was able to survive this, and this event has shaped the culture of my company and the way we have done business ever since.

FROM GROWTH MODE TO SURVIVAL MODE

The first decade I was in business was all about growth. Then came the late 1980s, when, for the most part, the construction economy was very good. In the fiscal year of 1988–89, in fact, I made more money than I'd ever made in any previous year, and by quite a bit. Still, I was a young contractor and didn't have the wisdom or experience that a more mature contractor might have had. I hadn't been through many boom and bust cycles. When the industry is booming, you tend to think it's always going to be that good.

So, I took my earnings and leveraged them to grow the company. I added staff, bought equipment, and expanded on just about every front. Then, the next year (1989–90), things started turning. The late eighties had been a really vibrant period, with people expanding and developing their companies, and then all of a sudden we were overbuilt.

Soon, the construction economy tanked. By 1991–92, it was almost dead. The banks had extended way too much credit—and I had incurred too much debt. I was banking with five different banks, and I had $1 million of unsecured credit, which meant I could borrow $1 million and didn't have to collateralize it. It was like I had a $1 million credit card. I think back to that time and think about how young and inexperienced I was and the credit they gave me, and I think, "They must have been crazy!"

The crash was not as drastic as 2008, but for a small contractor like me, with as much debt as I was carrying, it was catastrophic. I had expanded the company primarily by leveraging the money I had and incurring debt, and all of a sudden the faucet turned off. I mean, it happened *quickly*. Garbutt Construction shifted from growth mode to survival mode.

I remember looking at my line of credit and thinking, "Man, I won't ever be able to pay this back." One particular day I went to all five banks with my accountant and my lawyer, sat down with them, and said, "We need for you folks to work with us. We're not sure how we're going to work our way out of this." I remember that day vividly.

I got various responses. Some of them worked with us and some of them didn't. We tried to satisfy the ones that wouldn't work with us, we took advantage of the arrangements we made with the others, and eventually they were all paid back. We didn't have to file for any kind of protection, no bankruptcy or anything. In a lot of ways, I'm prouder of that than I am of anything else I've done in business. Honest dealing and strict discipline pulled me out of the situation I had gotten into. That experience has shaped everything I have done in business from that time forward.

First, I know not to be leveraged. Cash is the oxygen you need to survive. You must have some stowed away for the hard times, because they come. For several years

Cash is the oxygen you need to survive. You must have some stowed away for the hard times, because they come.

now, we have had a line of credit—the bonding company likes to know you can go borrow money if you need to—but we haven't used it for almost a decade. So, I have been able to maintain my construction business with no significant debt.

More importantly, this experience forced me to quickly adapt in the face of changing circumstances—which is a good thing. Success in business—any business, but especially construction—requires adaptability to change. The forty years that I have been in business have seen many changes. Some changes, like the early 1990s economic situation, are bad,

Success in business—any business, but especially construction—requires adaptability to change.

and a company and its culture must be resilient. There are also good changes, which have certainly taken place in construction over the last forty years. Good or bad, though, change requires a company culture that can adapt.

YOU CAN'T DO IT LIKE YOU USED TO DO

The methods used by owners of buildings or buyers of construction services to procure those services—to hire contractors—have changed drastically in the last forty years. These changes have been improvements, but they have also required that companies change the way they operate, their culture. Contractors can't do things the way they were done when I got started.

When I first got my start, all I had to do then was have enough in the bank to bond the job and make a bid, and, if I was the lowest bidder, the job was mine. My funds were limited, though, which limited my bonding capacity and, therefore, the type of jobs I could bid on. Starting from scratch like Garbutt Construction meant doing smaller jobs. For my first job, in fact, the business was just *me*, so I did almost everything myself. I had come back home to Dublin and decided I was going to start my construction business. I had saved up about $2,500, which is grossly inadequate to start a construction business. Had I known that at the time, I probably wouldn't have done it. I guess, looking back, it's a good thing I didn't know.

I really didn't want to be a house builder. I had always wanted to be in commercial construction. As I mentioned, though, to be in commercial construction, you had to provide a payment and performance bond, and to provide a payment and performance bond, you had to have some assets, which I didn't have. In fact, you needed to have liquid assets, which I *certainly* didn't have. The rule of thumb was that for every ten-dollar bond for construction, you had to have at least a dollar of liquid assets.

So there I was, wanting to be in commercial construction, and some local doctors in Dublin were wanting to build an addition to their office. My father owned a drug store, so he had to interface with a lot of doctors, and these doctors gave me the opportunity to bid. This was a private job, so they could restrict, meaning they weren't required to let anybody and everybody bid. The job was $93,000, which meant I needed about $9,000 of liquid assets to bid the job.

So, my father gave me $10,000. He said, "Son, that's all you're getting. If it goes fine, good. If you fall flat on your face, well, you've had your opportunity." I couldn't spend that money; it had to sit there. But it allowed me to bid the job, which ended up being Garbutt Construction's first job. I was the estimator. I was the superintendent. I was pretty much most of the labor!

It got scary after I poured the concrete slab because that was the night that the temperature went down to twelve degrees. Now, concrete can freeze, and if it freezes, it's just no good. That's a big waste. So the two concrete finishers I had hired and I put out salamander heaters and stayed with it all night long, but we did it, and the concrete didn't freeze.

That was the first job I ever did. Those doctors gave me the opportunity, and it turned out well. But it could have gone very badly. The construction world was pretty cutthroat at the time, and if I had lost money due to something like the concrete freezing, my journey would have been over before it even started.

DESIGN-BID-BUILD AND ITS DANGERS

The model that all construction service delivery operated on at that time is known as the "design-bid-build" model of construction service delivery. The way the design-bid-build process works is an architect designs a building or renovation and (supposedly) furnishes the contractor with all the information he needs to put a bid on the building. So, if you have a multitude of contractors and they're all working based on that same contract document, those same drawings and specifications, you should get

On a construction project, the general contractor or construction manager hires various subcontractors, who run their own companies with their own crews that specialize in a specific construction trade or discipline.

the same end product, no matter who builds it. The contractor with the lowest bid gets the job.

In other words, the mind-set or the basic assumption is that construction is a commodity, and there is no difference between Contractor A and Contractor B, other than price. This is far from true. Just as the difference between a Chevrolet and a Cadillac is in more than just their price, there is a contrast between the service, qualifications, and quality you get from different contractors. Each contractor is individual.

For that reason and others, sophisticated buyers have discovered that the design-bid-build model is fraught with peril, for both contractors and the people buying their services, for the following reasons.

When you, Mr. Contractor, have to bid on a certain day and by a certain time, your price has to be in *at that time*—if the time is 2:00, and your bid is in at 2:01, your bid is rejected. On the other hand, any price put out early runs the risk of being undercut. So, contractors don't want to make their bids too early, either.

This also applies to the subcontractors that the general contractor will hire to do the job and who he needs pricing information from to make his bid. No subcontractor is going to call you two weeks ahead and say, "My electrical price is going to be $100,000," because then they are at risk of having it *shopped.* That is, the general contractor might then go to another electrical subcontractor and say, "Brand X gave me $100,000 on the electrical. You need to beat it if you want the job." That's called shopping a price, and it goes on a good bit. So, nobody puts their price out until just before the bid.

If you're a contractor and you're putting a bid together, prices from subcontractors don't start coming in until maybe an hour before the bid. You may even be getting prices up to seconds before the bid. The contractor has to put all this together—he's going to get the job based on what his price is. So, Mr. Contractor, you may get a price five minutes before bid time, and it may be considerably low. Why is it so low? Maybe that subcontractor has left something out that he doesn't realize will be a cost. Maybe the sub is inexperienced and doesn't know what he's doing. Maybe the subcontractor is taking too big a risk with the price because he needs the work. There are all sorts of reasons.

You may not know who that subcontracting company is or anything about it, except that it has the cheapest price; and you know that probably, if you don't use it, one of your competitors will. You're in the dilemma of making the decision whether to use that price in your bid or not. And you have to make that decision in the span of five minutes.

You may have just spent the last two or three weeks putting all these prices together and doing all the work to quantify all the materials and so on, and then at the last minute you have some yahoo that you don't know anything about who's bidding thousands of dollars low: "Do I use it or do I not use it?" If you use it, that price may not be valid, but you've just put your number out there and you've bonded it. You have to live with that number you put out there.

All contractors at one point in time have used a price they shouldn't have used, used a subcontractor they shouldn't have used, or left out something that they should have included—and yet they have put their assets at risk to bond the job. When you bid a job, you have to provide a bid bond. The purpose of the bid bond is to say, "We're going to honor our price." If you present a bid bond and for some reason you refuse to sign the contract, then the bonding company is on the hook for 5 percent of the cost of the project.

Early on, just a few months after starting my business, I was the low bidder on a school renovation. After finding out, I discovered that we had left out the acoustical ceiling—a cost of about $15,000. Today, that doesn't sound like much, but back then, that was a pretty significant price, and basically, based on the bid, we were going to make *very little* if we had to absorb the fact that we left that out.

We had the option to go to the owner and say, "Okay, we left the ceiling out and we can't, or don't want to, do the job. So, we're not going to sign the contract," which would have meant the forfeiture of our bid bond. Forfeiting on a bid bond is the kiss of death for a contractor. It's like a scarlet letter. It will be hard to get somebody to bond you from then on. So, we made the decision that we were going to do the job. If we didn't make any money, or even if we lost money, then that's just what we were going to have to do.

With a low bid, a smart contractor will figure out ways to cut costs, get some lower prices, and pick up extra money along the way. We did the job, and we came out ahead. It wasn't as bad as we had thought it would be, but we had to swallow hard and make that decision. We were just starting, so, if I had lost money, it would have been pretty traumatic. It would have probably been life threatening. We had to say, "All right. We're going to do whatever it takes to finish this project and try to minimize the damage of it."

That's the way the system worked up until people who were sophisticated buyers of construction figured out, "This is a crazy way to do business," because they got poor quality. That's why the design-bid-build model is also risky for buyers. If somebody is going to live and die on a price that was too cheap to begin with, then that person has to try to cut every corner he can to be able to provide the project as cheaply as he can. That comes through in the quality of the product.

THE NEW CULTURE OF CONSTRUCTION

Design-bid-build was the MO for commercial construction until recently, especially in the public sector. Private-sector owners had already begun to realize, "There's got to be a better way," but in the public sector, the mind-set was still, "We've got to look out for the taxpayer, and we don't want to pay any more than we have to for these builders." That mind-set has also changed recently, though, and this affects the culture of the industry. Quality construction firms must be up-to-date in their culture in order to adapt to the current environment.

In the past fifteen or twenty years, Georgia has been reforming its procurement laws. One of the changes is that now the state can award contracts on the basis of considerations other than price. This pretty much replaces the design-bid-build model with a qualifica-tions-based selection process. This opened up the way for the delivery systems of design-build and construction management (though the design-bid-build, or hard bid, model still gets used). The opening up of these new delivery systems was a real milestone for us because now 95 percent of what we do is done differently from the design-bid-build model and according to one of these other two models.

With these models, we are selected based on our qualifications, not necessarily our price. As a matter of fact, when we're selected, the design may not have even started. The buyers don't even know what the building looks like. They may have a budget, and we may be responsible for helping the designer make sure he designs to that budget. There are two ways this can happen.

The first is called the *design-build model*. In this model, there is a partnership between the general contractor and the architect who designs the building. The design partner, the architect, typically works as a subcontractor, hired by the general contractor. When we do design-build, we hire the architect, we pay the architect, and *we* are the architect's client. The building owner, or buyer of construction services, has a single contract with one party—the general contractor, or 'design builder.'

In *construction management*, the second model, the building owner or buyer of construction services hires the architect, pays the architect, and is the design firm's client. The buyer has two separate contracts: one with the design firm and one with the general contractor.

In both cases, the contractor is on the team virtually from day one. In these processes, we, the contractors, test the architect's design according to what it will cost, since the general contractor is the expert on the costs of construction. We also evaluate the design for constructability. An architect may come up with a very creative design, but it's no good if it is impossible to build. So, when we do a design-build or a construction management job, we are the budget experts, we are the constructability experts, and we are advising that design team and that owner about cost as well as practicality of the design.

This is all very different from just having the lowest price, and it ends up benefitting the owner or buyer, who gets a higher-quality design and a more thoroughly developed budget, which increases efficiency and helps prevent unexpected costs from popping up down the road.

Each of the two models has its good and bad qualities from the perspective of the contractor. Design-build tends to be more collaborative. Because we pay them and we're their client, we have more control over the architect or design firm. They can't say, "You don't tell us what to do. We're not working for you. We're working for the owner." On the other hand, there is more risk in the design-build because, if the project gets designed poorly, the buck stops with us. In the construction management process, if a design is faulty, then we don't incur that liability, but in design-build, we do. We have to carry additional insurance in the design-build process because we have some liability that we otherwise wouldn't have.

First and foremost, though, both models are based on collaboration, which also happens to be one of the key aspects of Lean construction and greatly improves the process for both the contractor and the buyer. We now use pull planning (which I'll explain in chapter 5) not only on the jobsite but in pre-construction, as well. That means we have to get the architect or design firm involved and make sure they are on board with the Lean culture that we have implemented. This works well in the design-build model, since the architect is accountable to us. With construction management, we need to go even further and get the owner to buy in to the process and culture in order for effective collaboration to take place.

As I will explain in the chapters ahead, collaboration among these parties benefits the job as a whole by increasing productivity, efficiency, and quality, which is good both for the folks working on the project and for the person paying for it.

These new ways of approaching a construction project are all matters of culture. For that reason, in this new environment, a firm must have an up-to-date and flexible culture in order to produce quality in the current environment. Lean, I have found, is the most effective way to develop this kind of culture.

DEBUNKING THE CONVENTIONAL WISDOM

You may have heard the old saying, "Cheap, good, and fast—pick any two." In other words, you can have high quality, you can have a low price, or you can build productively and efficiently, but you can't have all three. They're mutually exclusive, to some degree. This was definitely the traditional wisdom in the construction industry.

We Do Three Types of Jobs Here...
GOOD, FAST AND CHEAP
You May Choose Any Two!

If It Is Good and Cheap
It Will Not Be Fast.

If It Is Good and Fast
It Will Not Be Cheap.

If It Is Fast and Cheap
It Will Not Be Good.

One of my goals with Garbutt Construction, and with Lean, is to debunk that idea. With Lean methods and culture in place, a firm can actually deliver quality, economy, and efficiency in a construction project. Toyota showed that you can build a product efficiently and economically and still have it come out good quality. I think we can show the same thing in construction. By eliminating waste—another key Lean idea—you can construct a quality building or other project by means of a productive, economical, and time-efficient process.

> *With Lean methods and culture in place, a firm can actually deliver quality, economy, and efficiency in a construction project.*

Getting things right and achieving a high standard of quality in construction have always been central principles at Garbutt Construction. They are built into our core values, and they have been reflected in some of the major projects we have worked on, both before and after our adoption of Lean culture. In the next chapter, I describe one of the biggest jobs we have ever done, the Old Governor's Mansion on the campus of Georgia College in Milledgeville, Georgia. This historic restoration illustrates the commitment to quality that animates our culture and values.

CHAPTER TWO

A COMMITMENT TO QUALITY

Even though we were working on an existing building, not building one from scratch, the Old Governor's Mansion was, at the time, our company's biggest job: putting twenty-first-century infrastructure into a nineteenth-century building. A job of that kind means a lot of details, as well as lots of collaboration among a lot of subcontractors. The job doesn't go well unless you have strong relationships. It's kind of like building a ship in a bottle.

Historical restoration, the process of restoring a building as close as possible to what it looked like at a certain time in history, always requires special attention and a commitment to quality. The National Park Service has established high standards for the historic preservation of buildings that are going to be National Historic Landmarks or are going to be on the National Register of Historic Places. We have evolved into specialists in this over the course of the life of our company. We are also specialists in the kind of collaborative and relationship-building work that these projects require.

The mansion, which was the Governor's Mansion for the state of Georgia before and during the Civil War, has been on the National Register of Historic Places since 1970, so special care was taken with this project to ensure that we were doing high-quality work. This project also illustrates another important part of the journey and the evolution of Garbutt Construction: the relationships we have developed and the partners who have influenced us along the way.

The Old Governor's Mansion job went well because, to accomplish the detailed historical restoration, we had to first build strong relationships.

BUILDING RELATIONSHIPS

In 2001, when the restoration of the Old Governor's Mansion was in the works, the state of Georgia had earmarked it as a project that they wanted to do as a construction management project because they wanted to make the selection based on qualifications. The state had chosen Lord Aeck Sargent, a major Atlanta firm, as the architectural firm. The preference of Lord Aeck Sargent for a general contractor was to have the Christman Company out of Lansing, Michigan, involved in the project. Christman has been around for more than a hundred years and has a stellar historical restoration division. The state, however, wanted a firm from Georgia (frankly, they didn't want a Yankee to do it).

Our involvement occurred thanks to a network of relationships. One of the principals in the firm of the Christman Company consulted with Lord Aeck Sargent to see if they could give them a recommendation on a Georgia contractor, and Tony Aeck, who is one of the principals of Lord Aeck Sargent, consulted with Lane

Greene, an old architect friend of mine, because he knew Lane had done some historic projects in Georgia.

We had over the years done a few projects with Lane Greene. Lane was a one-man architectural firm, but he also did a lot of historical restoration work and was well respected in historical restoration circles. Lane recommended us, so we were on board.

The Governor's Mansion was our largest collaborative effort on a project up to that time, involving two general contractors, a design firm, the curator of the property, the board of regents for the University System of Georgia, and Georgia College itself. Everyone had their handprints on this thing, even before getting the subcontractors involved.

Considering how complicated it was, the project went extremely well, and this was thanks to the deep collaboration among the players involved, which resulted in lasting relationships. Garbutt Construction and the Christman Company continued their relationship for several years, even cofounding an LLC, and we still have a close working relationship with Lord Aeck Sargent. Our relationship with Georgia College and State University has continued to be significant, as well. We have been their restoration contractor for most of the old college buildings on campus.

So, out of that one major project came some very productive relationships for us. Also, the Old Governor's Mansion raised our profile a great deal, since we were working alongside a major national firm and did award-winning work on a recognizable property and institution. It took us from being a local contractor to having high credibility as one of the premier historical restoration firms in the state.

The root of all of this was our relationship with Lane Greene. We had built up a relationship of trust with Lane Greene where he was comfortable in recommending us, and later established a relationship with Christman that lasted years. Relationships like this, as well as relationships we have developed through Associated General Contractors (AGC), have been central to the development of Garbutt Construction's culture and commitment to quality.

WHAT WE VALUE MOST

Not long after the Old Governor's Mansion project, we decided to keep working on this development by participating in an industry peer group sponsored by AGC. More than ten years ago, AGC started networking contractors that were similar in size and in market but weren't competitors, and they provided facilitators for each group.

We joined a group of six or seven contractors who get together twice a year and share stories and ideas about our businesses. We are still a part of this group. Each member is a little different, but we all share similarities. We've bonded as friends, but we've also had a lot of common struggles and victories. It has been helpful to have a group like that to run things by, get advice from, and consult with. That's been part of our growth.

When our group first started meeting a decade ago, we talked about all aspects of the construction business, problems we had encountered and maybe solved, strategies, financials—the good, the bad, and the ugly. We did a pretty thorough audit of everybody's business.

One of the first things the AGC facilitator asked us was, "Do you have a strategic plan? Everybody should have one." Well, none of us did, so that became number-one at the top of all our to-do lists. I had to figure out how to get my arms around this idea of a strategic plan, so I read a book that another one of the contractors recommended to me: *Mastering the Rockefeller Habits,* by Verne Harnish.[2] That book provides a process and template for developing a one-page strategic plan, and we use that model to this day to develop our own strategic plan.

In first developing our strategic plan, the core values were the first thing we dealt with, and I think that's the right approach. You must decide who you are, or at least who you want to be as a company, and what things make you who you are—and those things, those core values, should never change. Everything else in business changes, but core values should be what you test everything by. Every decision you make, every action you take, every person you hire ought to be tested by your core values. They must be lived from top to bottom.

I'm not sure we exemplified all those core values when we started, but we *wanted* to. We spent two days hammering them out, and they have stayed that way for ten years. They've served us well. We've tried to embed them in everything we do so that they are part of the fabric of the company. We try to keep them in everybody's consciousness as much as we can. We talk about them every day. We have awards for people who exemplify them, we put them on T-shirts, we put them in presentations, and we do our best to live up to them.

Relationships—within the company, with partners, with owners—are so central to our culture that they tie all of our core values together. All of our five core values have to do with building and strengthening relationships in some way. They also, as you'll see, can be seen as components of a Lean culture.

---

2   Verne Harnish, *Mastering the Rockefeller Habits* (Ashburn, VA : Gazelles, Inc., 2002).

1. DO WHAT YOU SAY WHEN YOU SAY

One of the things you learn pretty early on in the construction business is that if you can earn the reputation of doing what you say you will do when you say you will do it, then you're going to separate yourself from 95 percent of the rest of the industry. People come to appreciate that.

To do this means promising only what can be delivered—don't overestimate what you can get done—and then, once you've committed to that, hold yourself accountable to following through.

None of the core values is more important than the others, but this is probably the one I focus on most on a daily basis. When somebody we work with, whether it's one of our people in the company or one of our subcontractors, commits to doing something and then follows through on it, doing whatever it takes to meet that commitment, we make sure to recognize and reward that.

This value is also a major component of Lean because, on a construction project, everybody is affected by what everyone else is doing. All the players are linked, so when somebody commits to doing something by a certain date or time and then doesn't do it, it has a ripple effect through the whole project. So, making the commitment to what you're going to do and following through on meeting that commitment has a huge impact on the project, the schedule of the project, and the efficiency and productivity of the project.

I've never actually hired contractors until I bought a house a year and a half ago, and after the process of having some very minor work done, I understood why "doing what you say when you say" is important! Not only do most people not do what they say they're going to do, but you also start to appreciate the ones who are at least telling you why they can't do what they said they were going to do. Most people don't do what they say, and then they don't follow up, and you never know what happened to them until you run them down. So the ones that actually did what they said they were going to do, and if they didn't, told me why—those are the ones I didn't mind working with.

—J. Charlie Garbutt, Vice President of Marketing

2. LIVE THE GOLDEN RULE

This one sort of speaks for itself. It includes treating others with the same respect that you expect from them, and the importance of demonstrating empathy and understanding.

How does it tie into the management of construction, though? Well, construction projects always have a lot of people working alongside one another who have to coordinate their activities. One of the things Lean accomplishes is that it brings various parties, especially individual subcontractors, out of their silos, so to speak. Typically, especially for the ones who are operating the same way they always have, the main focus of a subcontractor on a construction project is singularly on what they have to do: getting it done, and being as productive as they can in a very narrow lane. The electrician is just interested in getting his work done; the plumber is interested in getting his work done; and so on down the line, with not much consideration for all the other disciplines.

With Lean, and especially pull planning, the electrician sees on a clearer basis how what he does affects the heat and air conditioning contractor, for instance. They start collaborating, and one of them says, "Well, if you could do it this way, that would allow me to go ahead and do this, and that means I could be a whole lot more productive." Then they start cooperating back and forth and look at the project more holistically.

Soon the plumber figures out, "If I can help the HVAC contractor today, and I need help from him tomorrow, he's probably going to do unto me like I do unto him." He helps out, and everybody gets more productive. So, there is a practical and Lean aspect of the Golden Rule in the workings of a construction project: If you can get folks to come out of those silos and collaborate and cooperate, then it doesn't take them long to figure out, "Hey, this is a better way to do it, and if I help this guy, he'll help me, and it'll be a win-win for both of us sooner or later."

Have you ever worked on a Habitat for Humanity project? If so, you'll recognize the way people tend to approach them with a real "What can I do?" attitude, and it's amazing to see those houses go up so fast because everyone is being unselfish and wants to help the other guy. If you can get that attitude established on a construction project, you have a Golden Rule kind of attitude, and that's when you really see some good stuff happen.

Trying to create a Lean culture in construction is really about managing an open and collaborative team, making sure that everybody trusts everybody else on the team not to be just looking after their self-interest, but looking out for the best interest of the project as a whole, or the common good, and building those relationships is the backbone of that. A lot of subcontractors just want to get in and get out, and they really don't care about the overall project, but they do know how the rest of the project impacts them. When we're in a scheduling meeting and we're questioning our subcontractors' approaches or techniques, they can see that we live the Golden Rule: we do unto others as we would have them do unto us, and then they feel a little more comfortable in opening up and thinking outside of the box.

—Sean Moxley, President

I apply the Golden Rule not only when I interact with subcontractors but also when I interact with owners. If we need to make a change in the way we're doing something, or if we run into a struggle on a job, then we can be better contractors if we put ourselves in the owner's shoes. Also, if you treat the owner the way you want to be treated—for example, being honest and giving them a credit when you find out you've over-budgeted for something—then that owner is more likely to help you out down the road and work with you if you've under-budgeted.

—Chris Davis, Project Manager

3. BE RELATIONSHIP FOCUSED WITH EMPLOYEES, CUSTOMERS, AND PARTNERS

Again, we value relationships above all, and this third core value focuses on listening when others speak and valuing what they have to say. When you do this, you develop relationships characterized by *trust*. We aim for trust in all our relationships, whether it's within the company, with clients, or with partners like the ones we worked with on the Old Governor's Mansion. Once you establish one of these relationships, doing business gets a whole lot easier and goes a whole lot faster. Garbutt Construction has done very well with repeat business, which to my mind is due mainly to this core value. We've been able to establish relationships of trust with our clients.

Good relationships are just as crucial on a jobsite where you have as many as thirty different individual companies as subcontractors in various disciplines and trades. If they come together once a week with a common initiative and a common goal, then they form relationships, and typically they become pretty good friends. They're thrown in the same room once a week, and they've got to brainstorm and collaborate to come up with a way to work together for the good of the project. That's relationship-building in and of itself.

It's like a football team. The goal is to get the ball to the goal line, but there's blocking, and there's tackling, and there's running, and there's passing; and these are all components that must work together. The team has to come together to make it work. If everybody's focused on getting the ball across the goal line, then the team gels, and it almost forces them to build relationships, which is amazing.

4. WHATEVER IT IS, DO IT RIGHT

We sum this one up like this: Pursue excellence in everything you do, and take pride in delivering quality with integrity. I like to think of this one in terms of the tortoise and the hare. The hare goes quickly, but then stalls, or has to retrace his steps, and ends up not getting things done right. The hare approach may seem appealing, but in construction it often means work has to be redone or is not done to as high a standard of quality as we aim for. We go much more for the tortoise approach: a steady and reliable rhythm that delivers quality results. We work at achieving this through the Lean practices that I discuss in later chapters.

The core values are all of the same importance, but one that is particularly meaningful to me and that connects well to Lean is "whatever it is, do it right"—because if you don't do it right, then you have to do it again. That is a lot of time, a lot of waste. We have some superintendents who do what they say when they say, and they will get it done, which is good. Our clients appreciate that. On the other hand, those people who do it very fast sometimes end up not doing it correctly.

—J. Charlie Garbutt, *Vice President of Marketing*

Our approach has always been, "Whatever it is, do it right." This one is fresh on my mind because of an addition we built recently. After we turned the building back over to the owner, a plumbing issue came up in the existing building that was outside the scope of work for the project. It would've been very easy to say, "Well, that wasn't part of the scope of work and for us to address that issue is going to cost you an additional" whatever it would be to fix the issue. In this case, it required cutting up a slab, redoing some plumbing lines under the existing slab, and redoing all the finishes in the surrounding area to fix it. We had a lot of conversation about it, and (going back to our core value of living the Golden Rule) we felt like it was our duty to go in and fix it.

> *So, unfortunately, sometimes problems aren't found right away, and that sometimes means things are covered up and don't become an issue until it's really tough to fix them. Still, if fixing a problem is going to mean tearing up concrete or ripping down sheet rock, it's worth doing to make sure that it was done right, even if it's something that was caused by some other party, or whatever the case may be. We feel like it's worth it to make sure that the end product is a high-quality product.*
>
> **—Sean Moxley, President**

5. BE OPEN AND RECEPTIVE

This value requires exercising patience and positivity under all circumstances, as well as the seeking of opportunities for collaboration and seeing value in everyone's contribution. One of the central aspects of Lean is the idea that the brain-power or the talents of multiple people will almost always give you a better solution than if you're relying on one person's idea.

That doesn't mean the original idea is not good. But that good idea can be a catalyst for other ideas, including ideas about how to improve on the original. I've seen this happen on a lot of occasions in the weekly pull-planning session on projects. Someone will suggest the way they would do a particular task, and someone else will say, "Yeah, but what would happen if we did it this other way?" If the first person is negative and tends to take the attitude that, "We've never done it that way before," or, "That's different from how I usually do things," he will resist; but if he *is* open and receptive, the whole group will start playing off each other's ideas, and I've seen some pretty amazing things happen as a result.

On a recent project, for example, the sprinkler contractor was struggling to work around the HVAC guy, and his solution was going to be to just pull off of the project for three or four weeks, then come back and do his work after the HVAC was finished. This would have delayed the job as a whole. When somebody pulls off of a project, it can be very difficult to get them back on. You want all of your contractors to be able to come to the job and continuously work.

So, we got the sprinkler contractor to stay in the planning session long enough to brainstorm ideas, and he was receptive when someone asked, "What if you start over here instead of over there?" even though that was not the way he typically did things. So, we refined that idea. Even the electrician offered some suggestions, and he didn't even have a dog in the fight. By the end of the session, we had it figured out and the sprinkler contractor didn't have to get off of the job, and we avoided the delay and stayed productive. And it just started with one idea that got perfected over the course of the conversation.

A CORE-VALUES-BASED STRATEGY

After we established our core values, it was up to us to develop a long-term strategic plan—a living, breathing, growing plan telling us where we wanted to go and how we wanted to go about getting there. Already, at this point in our journey, we had begun embodying the Lean value of continuous improvement: Our overall aim was to continue to grow as a company offering construction services of the highest quality in our region. Our strategic plan was geared toward offering the best, and Lean has become a central part of that plan and that pursuit of quality.

The strategic plan, unlike the core values, changes over time. It starts with the question of what big accomplishment the company as a whole is aiming for—that's your BHAG (big, hairy, audacious goal), which is an idea from Jim Collins.[3] This is the top of the mountain for the company. Boil this down to a three-to-five-year goal that will start getting you there. Then you ask, "If I want to hit this three-to-five-year goal, what do I need to be doing every year between now and then?" There's your annual goal, and you figure out what needs to happen this quarter in order to hit that annual goal—so everything should align.

We have an annual strategic planning meeting where we develop our strategic plan for the year, decide who in the company is going to be the champion for each of the goals we're trying to accomplish, and figure out on a quarterly basis what needs to happen to hit those goals and who is going to be responsible for achieving those quarterly aims. By doing this, we can hold ourselves and each other accountable for what we're trying to accomplish, and we can measure how

---

3   Jim Collins and Jerry Poras, *Built to Last: Successful Habits of Visionary Companies* (New York: HarperCollins Publishing, 1994).

we're doing when we meet again at the end of the quarter, and so on down the line.

If this was all in a big, voluminous manual, it would be very ineffective. As I mentioned, we use Verne Harnish's one-page strategic plan. Everything is written on one page, and we blow it up to poster size and put it out there for everyone in the company to see, so everyone knows where we're trying to go, what we're trying to accomplish in the short term, and what our long-term goals are. At the end of the process, not only are all the company goals aligned, but the people responsible for them are all aligned, as well.

I think we were the first in our peer group to really take the importance of strategic planning to heart, and it has paid dividends for us. We've been doing this process, annually and quarterly, for over ten years now. We've stayed loyal to our commitment to strategic planning, and it has allowed us to keep raising the bar, to maintain continuous improvement in the company. We had had great success on the Old Governor's Mansion just prior to first formulating our strategic plan, and at the time, we were determined to take on more projects of that scale, and independently of a larger general contractor. Since then, we've been able to continue to offer the best on large and small projects, including projects that are possibly even more ambitious than the Old Governor's Mansion.

CHAPTER THREE

ENCOUNTERING AND IMPLEMENTING LEAN

After the Old Governor's Mansion, our next big job, the way I like to think about it, was like falling dominoes: We set everything up carefully at the front end of the process, we implemented the plan, and all the pieces fell into place, one after another. It was a thing of beauty to watch how well this complex project came together, and it was all thanks to Lean: this job, the Old First National Bank building in downtown Dublin, Georgia, was the first large-scale project for which we employed Lean methods.

Once again, we found ourselves having to put twenty-first-century infrastructure into an old building that hadn't been designed to accommodate it. This time, it wasn't a nineteenth-century building; it was built in 1911. In that sense, this project was even more ambitious than the Old Governor's Mansion had been.

Our work on Old First National was not historical restoration, but rather *adaptive reuse*. The building had originally been a bank and professional office building, and we were preparing it for use in higher education (as the campus for Georgia Military College). This meant installing HVAC—the building wasn't originally air conditioned—and a new electrical system. Since this would be a twenty-first-century educational institution, we needed to add an elaborate system for data sharing and wireless internet throughout the building, as well. This challenge meant a lot of work, a lot of subcontractors, and a lot of careful planning. Lean made a world of difference for this project, by bringing all of the players together in the scheduling process and maximizing productivity so that we were able to do good work within the budget and time frame expected—everything falling right into place.

LEAN ENLIGHTENMENT

In the lead-up to taking on this project, I encountered the idea of the twenty-mile march. In construction, this idea basically takes the planning of a project to the day-to-day level and works very well with Lean planning methods by getting workers to think about what they accomplish in the space of a day. I started thinking about daily planning in terms of twenty-mile marches after seeing Jim Collins talk about Amundsen at a conference in Atlanta, Georgia.

In *Great By Choice,* business guru Jim Collins tells the story of Roald Amundsen, the Antarctic explorer who was the first to reach the South Pole, beating his rival Robert Falcon Scott in 1911.[4] The story of Amundsen's victory and Scott's failure is partly a tortoise and hare story. One key element of Amundsen's strategy was the goal of marching twenty

---

4   Jim Collins and Morten Hansen, *Great By Choice: Uncertainty, Chaos, and Luck* (New York: HarperCollins, 2011).

miles per day and no more, an ambitious but realistic goal. On days when it was easily achieved, his team stopped at the twenty-mile mark in order to conserve their energy.

Most days, he'd be able to meet that, and by not overdoing it, he and his men had energy for the days when travel was tougher. Slow and steady. And this won the race. Scott would push his men as far as he could on any given day, tried to make up lost time when bad weather had slowed them down, and stopped altogether when the going got tough or weather was bad. They made it to the South Pole much later than Amundsen, and they died on the trip back.

The twenty-mile march represents a goal you have for a particular day—you set your stake in the ground, and that's what you aim to accomplish. Planning around twenty-mile marches makes you break things down and look at where your major milestones are and what your time frame is for reaching them—kind of like a day-by-day version of the strategic plan I talked about in the last chapter. Some days, hitting that goal might be a piece of cake, some days it might be a real challenge, but you figure out how to make it happen every day. If you don't get there, you look hard at what went wrong and figure out how to do things differently next time around.

If you have a bunch of work sitting there, and there's tangible stuff to be done, the human inclination is to do as much as you possibly can, and you think that's effective, but, really, someone who works with a set pace per day is much more productive than someone who always lives with, "I've got to get all this done right now."

—J. Charlie Garbutt, Vice President of Marketing

As I mentioned, Collins's ideas fit in perfectly with the Lean concepts that I was in the process of learning about and thinking about implementing at that time.

I have been a member of Associated General Contractors (AGC) for forty years, but about ten years ago I began to see things about Lean in the construction industry, and I was very curious about it. In particular, at one AGC conference I saw that there was a guy on the program from the Lean Construction Institute (LCI). This was the first time I'd ever heard of Lean—in fact, it may have been the first connection between AGC and the LCI. It piqued my interest. I didn't understand what it was, or what it was all about, but I started seeking out presentations on Lean at conferences. A year or so after my first exposure, I went to my first seminar on Lean at an AGC conference.

Lean began doing workshops at the national level of AGC, and that is where I got my most specific exposure. AGC has a Lean curriculum with seven units. I have taken all seven, passed the certification exam, and am now certified to teach Lean. I now teach it to all of my project managers and superintendents. I am also a member of the LCI, and I participate in Lean training programs.

SETTING UP THE DOMINOES

At the time of the First National Bank project, though, I was still going through this education process. My exposure to Jim Collins's ideas tied in with this perfectly—the twenty-mile march itself is a very Lean concept in that it regulates and streamlines work processes to maximize productivity. Collins also explains that successful business leaders shoot rifles before they shoot cannonballs. In other words, you don't bet the farm on something before trying it on a small scale. If you have a new idea, you do a model, sort of an incubator for the new idea, to see if it works. If it does, then you really pour the coals to it—you shoot the cannonballs.

This fit in exactly with our approach to Lean. We first tried it on a small hardscape project—that is, an outdoor project pouring sidewalks and plazas. We had sidewalks to put in all over our town, Dublin. This was our rifle shot. We had just two or three subcontractors on it.

I had been exposed to Lean, and I had heard the Jim Collins story about the twenty-mile march, so I brought those two or three subcontractors in, and we collaboratively figured out how much we could pour every day, and we set our goal to pour that much every day. At the start, we might be working until seven or eight at night to get it done, but, by the time we were at the end of the project, we were finishing the day's work by three or four o'clock.

For me, the lightbulb came on as I watched us get better every day, and I saw the value of setting those milestones and taking the collaborative Lean approach. I said, "You know, this stuff really works."

The question then was, "How will Lean work if you have thirty subcontractors?" So, that brings us back to the Old First National Bank building, which involved a lot of planning because it involved so many trades. We had data people, electrical people, sprinkler people, HVAC people, drywall people, painters. This was a very involved and complicated project. My superintendent, Tracy Lively, orchestrated it by breaking the project down into floors and deciding the sequence the floors would be worked on. Then we had the crews do their work on the floors in that sequence. So, for instance, the electricians had to be off of a floor and on to the next one in time for the sheet rock finishers to get onto that floor.

Tracy worked with all of the subcontractors to plan on a day-by-day basis how often each crew ought to be coming off those floors and how much work that would take each day from each crew. We brought a painter on months ahead of when they typically could get started. Painters usually like for everybody to be out of the way, for the job to be pretty much done. But we convinced the painter that he could start on one floor, when two floors down they might not even have it wired yet. This was a huge increase in productivity and efficiency.

So, it took careful planning, and each team knocked out a floor at a time, going up, like dominoes—and it worked *perfectly*. Seeing this domino effect in action gave us the confidence to say, "All right, we're embracing this. This is a system we're going to use."

My first encounter with Lean was the project that we did here in Dublin at Old First National Bank. Charlie had gone to the Lean construction training, had come back very enthusiastic about it, and floated this idea of the Last Planner® System, which at the time looked a lot to me like a typical three-week schedule that we had done, with the big difference that it involved the collaboration of all the subcontractors—in other words, it was a pull plan, as opposed to a push plan where we generate the schedule and dictate it to the subcontrac-

tors. We were building that schedule in a collaborative manner and pulling that information out of the guys that actually did the work.

—Sean Moxley, President

We had a great buy-in from the subcontractors on Old First National. Those meetings were so collaborative. While we were working on multiple stories, the actual footprint of the job was relatively small, so there was a good chance that there would've been people working on top of people. Through Lean and the pull planning, we were really able to keep that workflow just moving in a repetitious pattern. We moved from one level to the next, getting faster and more efficient as we went along.

—Chris Davis, Project Manager

CHAMPIONING LEAN CULTURE ON THE JOBSITE

The First National Bank building was the first major step in the company's journey toward embracing Lean culture along with the systems and methods that go with it. The biggest change was the introduction of the pull plan, which I will discuss in detail in chapter 5. Basically, this means the planning is more bottom-up and collaborative than top-down (a push plan). I anticipated it was going to take a lot more selling on my part to get my folks to embrace it, so I was on the site to make sure the launch of the plan went well, leading the planning sessions; but I was fortunate to have Tracy Lively as my superintendent and Chris Davis as project manager on that project, because Tracy and Chris immediately saw the value of it, and I just needed to get out of the way. After just a few weeks, they took it and ran with it, and got good results right away. Since then, my team has embraced it, and we've been able to do great things with it. Tracy and Chris are now true believers, and I expect they would tell you they wouldn't do another project without a pull plan.

> *Charlie is correct. I wouldn't do another job without a pull plan. Once you get your team involved, and once they see what you're doing and see the type of goals that you hit every week, these guys really get into it in the subcontractor meeting every week. They communicate more and better than I had ever seen before I started this Lean process.*
>
> **—Tracy Lively, Superintendent**

Tracy has been our Lean champion on the jobsite, and the new project managers we put with him, who may not have figured out how exactly to orchestrate it and make it work, learn a lot from seeing him in action. In particular, Tracy is a master of the twenty-mile march. He always sets ambitious goals. Some days, things go really well; some days, weather might be an impediment, or we don't have exactly what we need, and we've got to scramble to get it; but whatever it is, Tracy is a master at making it happen and getting it done. If he sets a goal, you'd better not bet against him.

I see things on Tracy's jobs all the time that he might not even think of as Lean. For instance, he keeps a very clean job. His housekeeping is excellent. A clean jobsite is usually a productive jobsite. You're not working around trash; you've got a good open space to work in. It makes people more productive.

Lean, to me, means a more productive jobsite, a safer jobsite, and more proactive interaction between the teams you have on a project. It makes the communication level really high between the men about the milestones we're trying to hit for that project.

Charlie brought me into it, but I take Lean seriously, and that's how I operate now. A lot of my contractors who were there when we were actually getting cranked up with it were involved, but I had a couple of them say it was b.s. Then, the more we got into it, the more these guys saw the value of it. Everybody just started clicking. On the last job I did, I had three or four trades that had never seen anything like that, and now they are the first ones that speak up in the meetings. You can just feel the energy in those meetings every week.

—Tracy Lively, Superintendent

Different contractors had more or less skepticism getting started, but I don't know anybody that, about midway through whatever job they are on, hasn't figured out, "Hey, this is a good thing. This not only helps the project—it helps us individually. We understand the big picture."

This effect doesn't even stop with the jobsite. It has had a ripple effect throughout our company and through the subcontractor corps. I have a student in a supervisor training program who was on a job with Tracy. Every week, he talks about that project and how much he learned.

I prefer to think of Lean as a whole as a matter of culture, rather than just as a system of methods or processes. Our path to Lean started very narrowly focused on the construction process, but in the broadest terms, Lean is about eliminating waste, which is a lot broader than just how you manage the construction site. It goes beyond the managing or building of a project into the internal operations of a company. At that level, it starts to become a mind-set, an attitude, about how you manage your business. What has happened to us now, I hope, is that we have bought in to the culture and taken the blinders off so that we can look at Lean processes that are beyond the management of the construction at the construction site.

I think our approach to Lean is something we're trying to get more holistic about. We're really focusing in on scheduling and different aspects of jobsites, using Lean on the jobsites, and definitely trying to take a more holistic approach in all processes company-wide to make us more Lean.

—Sean Moxley, President

Lean is a big cultural change. It challenges conventional wisdom in construction, and it has met some resistance. But it also addresses some of the problems that plague construction as it is currently practiced, and it improves on construction's ways of doing business. Lean emphasizes collaboration and careful planning, and it definitely works to increase productivity on the jobsite.

One of the most fundamental ideas and goals of Lean is the elimination of waste. This is where I'm going to start, because this remains one of the biggest problems the construction industry faces. It is also one of the places where our practices at Garbutt Construction are pushing ahead of traditional construction practices. The problem of waste makes it clear that Lean is a frontier in our region that we are at the very front of.

VALUE AND WASTE IN THE CONSTRUCTION INDUSTRY

Up until 2016, all of my exposure to Lean had been through Associated General Contractors (AGC). Recently, one of my Lean instructors recommended that I attend the annual conference for the Lean Construction Institute (LCI), which was in Chicago.

I had no idea how big this conference would be: There were 1,350 participants, far more than I had expected, and much bigger than any other conference I had ever been to. We filled the hotel—not just general contractors, but owners and buyers, architects, and various types of subcontractors.

Of the many general contractors involved, though, only three were from Georgia, and I knew the other two! Now, there are plenty of contractors in Georgia—hundreds. So, I recognized that being one of only three contractors there from the state of Georgia differentiated Garbutt Construction tremendously from its competitors in the region.

Georgia, though, is representative of the construction industry as a whole, especially in the Southeast. The industry here is behind and needs to catch up—especially small to mid-sized firms like ours. One way you can tell that construction is behind on Lean is in the amount of *waste*. A Lean jobsite is going to be one where there is much less waste, but flat productivity in the construction sector over the last several decades is accompanied by a lack of advances in waste reduction.

Productivity in manufacturing has nearly doubled, whereas in construction it has remained flat.

Overview of productivity improvement over time
Productivity (value added per worker), real, $ 2005

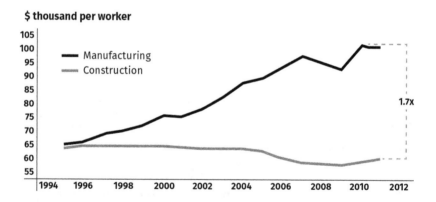

Source: Expert interviews; IHS Global Insight (Belgium, France, Germany, Italy, Spain, United Kingdom, United States); World Input-Output Database.
McKinsey & Company

LESS WASTE, MORE VALUE

One of the most basic principles of Lean is that, in everything you do on a very broad basis—building or making something, providing a service, whatever—you are doing one of two things: *Adding value* or *producing waste*. Waste is simply anything that doesn't add value. This certainly applies to construction. These categories cover everything in the construction process. Lean's approach is to encourage eliminating everything that does not add value—i.e., all waste. This increases productivity and profitability.

According to the original Lean theory of waste (which comes from Taiichi Ohno, chief engineer for Toyota), there are seven types of waste (or, in Japanese, seven *mudas*):

1. Overproduction
2. Waiting
3. Transporting
4. Inappropriate Processing
5. Unnecessary Inventory
6. Unnecessary/Excess Motion
7. Defects

Knowing these seven types of waste helps you know where to look to find and eliminate waste. Other Lean thinkers include an eighth category: Failing to fully use the knowledge or talents of workers. This is the product of insufficient collaboration.

When you start thinking in terms of the Lean theory of waste, you can find waste everywhere, from the jobsite to how you pay people, how you bill people, how paper flows in your company, and how your office is laid out. The goal is to get *everybody* in the mind-set of looking for it everywhere they can. This involves asking, about every process, "Is this adding value?" If it's not, then it's waste, and the question is, "How can I eliminate this waste?" Learning to see waste takes a training process.

Asking whether or not it adds value should be the acid test for everything you do. I think of adding value in terms of moving the ball. We're headed toward the goal line, and if we advance the ball down the field, then we have added value. If we haven't moved the ball, then what we have done is considered waste, and we need to figure out how to get rid of it. That's the very basic way to approach everything you do. You tend to see waste if you do that. You start questioning, "Well, why am I doing that? Am I moving *the ball*, or am I just moving?" If you're not attuned to it, or don't operate in a culture of seeking out waste to eliminate, then it's hard to see. That is a mindset that can make a dramatic difference if you can get everybody to buy in on it.

The problem of waste is such a big one that we even built it into our core values in the form of "Whatever it is, do it right." As I discussed earlier, nothing is more wasteful than having to do something over and over again because it wasn't done right the first time. If doing it right takes a little more time, that's still going to eliminate waste in the long run.

A construction project moves, like a river, from upstream to downstream. At the very beginning of the flow is the pre-construction design phase, and each step of the actual building process is downstream from that. The end of the stream comes with the delivery of the final project to the buyer. Some parts of the process, like pouring a foundation, are pretty far upstream—that is, they have to be done before a lot of the others can be. Painting, on the other hand, is pretty far downstream. Painters come in and work after everyone else is basically finished. The smoother this flow of activity and resources from upstream to downstream is, the less waste there is in the process.

Much of the waste that *is* generated comes from the flow between one part of the job to the others.

The type of waste I run into most often on a jobsite is a result of overproduction, which in this case means producing and delivering a product when it is not needed, or at least before it is needed, downstream. In fact, this is seen in Lean circles as the fundamental form of waste, because it has a tendency to give rise to all the others. For example, a concrete block or pallet of bricks adds value only when the mason is actually there on the site to lay it. If it is delivered before that point, it is just sitting there unnecessarily—it becomes unnecessary inventory—and is also an obstacle that has to be avoided or moved out of the way, producing unnecessary or excess motion.

Several years ago, however, we wouldn't have seen it this way. In fact, it is still a common practice to have all materials delivered up front, to be used as needed—"Just in Case." But this is a wasteful approach. There's a lot of wasted motion if you bring in too much material to the jobsite at one time because you have to stockpile it for when you need it. You end up having to move it around to get it out of the way. For example, coordinating the delivery of the drywall, like Tracy explains, is a big way to eliminate waste.

On every job, for example, I do a Lean planning session the week before we start drywall. We sit down as a team and figure out that we can have a truckload of drywall delivered to the site, say, every two days, and we won't have piles of drywall laying all over the building. To me, that's a Lean process.

To be honest with you, before I got introduced to Lean, I would have loaded this whole jobsite down with drywall. There would have been drywall stacked in every room. But then I got to understanding the purpose behind it, and it works.

—Tracy Lively, Superintendent

The philosophy behind having everything delivered up front is that you don't want to run out of material. There are two things you don't want to happen on the jobsite: 1) You don't want to have work waiting for workers to do it (upstream product waiting on downstream resources to make use of it), and 2) (what's even worse) you don't want workers hanging around without work to do (downstream resources waiting for upstream product to come flowing in). Some subcontractors are notorious for sending fifteen to twenty people to a site, when only ten or twelve are needed. If a superintendent has those extra men, he's as nervous as a cat on a hot tin roof. He has to balance the number of men he has with the amount of work that can be done on the site that day. It's a balancing act.

The solution to this is not the "Just in Case" approach, but instead "Just in Time" delivery—materials are delivered at precisely the time they are needed, and they don't clutter the jobsite, waiting around for weeks or even months to be put in place. The deliveries are also coordinated with the number of workers on the project on a specific day, so we don't have workers waiting on work.

As I'll discuss in later chapters, the pull plan really contributes to eliminating this type of waste. If all the contributors to a project are measuring when things need to be ready and when other things need to be done in light of what everyone else is doing on the jobsite, then materials can be delivered just in time to be used.

This is a point the construction industry needs to catch up on—there is still too much waste in the process.

HOW TO ELIMINATE WASTE

The elimination of waste, for Garbutt Construction, is typically driven by timing. We self-perform very little of our work. Our job in the construction process is to manage the various subcontractors who are actually doing the physical building work on the ground. If we can save time within the overall process, it reduces the cost of the project and is very much a benefit to the owner. On any given job, we've got a superintendent and project manager out there, along with a number of subcontractors, and every day that these folks are on the job is another day we have to pay them, which goes into the overall cost of the project. If one of my subcontractors spends time doing something that's not moving the ball, then that's not adding value: I'm buying something that I shouldn't be buying. If he eliminates that, then that money can go to the bottom line.

One of the most practical precepts of the Lean curriculum, and one that resonated with me very early on, is the idea that you're trying to eliminate workers waiting on work and work waiting on workers. If you never have workers waiting on anything—waiting on materials, waiting on approvals, waiting on other contractors to get out of the way—*and* if you never have work that is available to be done without the workers available to do it, then you've probably got the ultimate productive, efficient job. That, to me, is the ultimate elimination of waste. How is this achieved?

One technique for eliminating waste on the jobsite is called *assembly*. It's based on the idea that you can do better work in a controlled environment than you can on a jobsite. If you can build in an environment like a shop where the builders can do their best work, and then bring that assembly—doors, storefront, whatever—to the jobsite and set it right in place, that's very Lean.

The window man on my last job wanted to bring all his material out and build the windows on the jobsite. I said, "Negative. You build them in your shop, and I want you to bring however many you think you can do per day." That way I didn't have his material lying all over the place. Next, we worked together to figure out how many windows he could set per day, and that's what he brought in on a trailer per day for his guys to install.

If his materials were just sitting there, in the way and possibly getting damaged, that's a good example of waste, because then he has to turn around and build it all over again, doubling up the work, whereas if he brings it in, takes it right off the truck, and puts it in the hole, it's not just lying around. Everything was prepped by the time the windows arrived at the jobsite.

These subcontractors are also better equipped to build back at their shop than on the jobsite, which gives you better quality as well as more productivity. In this case, it was a three-day process, whereas before it would have been eight or ten days.

—Tracy Lively, Superintendent

A lot of the "Leaning" of a jobsite involves scheduling, which I'll talk about more in later chapters. You can get a lot of waste when you've got three or four specialty contractors waiting on another— for instance, when the plumber, the electrician, the sprinkler contractor, and the insulator are all waiting on the wall framer to get his wall up. If he says he's going to be through by a certain date, then they anticipate that they can go to work right after that, and if he's not, then you have to reschedule everything that the other folks are going to be doing, or figure out how they're going to work around that, which can be very wasteful.

Another technique Tracy is a master of is *resource leveling*. This has a lot to do with the rhythm of a job—that is, the steadiness of the flow from upstream to downstream. For example, you don't want four of your subcontractors working at a set pace and suddenly have one working at twice that pace (or half as fast, or assigning twice as many people as they need to do the work, etc.). A job ideally gets a rhythm: Once the electrician finishes work in his area, the plumber is ready to go in that area. Once a job gets in that rhythm, you want it to stay there. You want it to be steady and reliable, and that means keeping your resources—manpower and materials—balanced. If subcontractors are out of sync, you end up with waste. It doesn't actually do you any good to have one subcontractor running way out ahead of everyone else in terms of productivity, because that introduces too much variation, which means too much waste in the long run.

Remember the twenty-mile march. What you want is steady, continuous work where a piece is passed from one trade to another in a very reliable and methodical way. That means knowing day to day what size crew you need and what amount of materials, every step of the way.

On one job recently, my drywall man had sent seventeen guys to the site. I could tell it wasn't working; the rhythm was off. So I had him cut back to thirteen or fourteen guys—and these guys were able to hang a truckload of drywall every two days, instead of having seventeen guys install a truckload in a day and a half and then basically waste those resources for half a day.

Having a lot of people isn't always a good thing. For years, I thought it was. Years ago, I thought the more people I had on the job, the more the job was booming—but it really wasn't. I was stalling in different areas of the project that I wasn't seeing.

—Tracy Lively, Superintendent

The academic idea behind this resource leveling technique, and behind a lot of Lean scheduling, is Little's Law. If you work at a pace such that all of a sudden you have workers that are finished and don't have something to do, then you have workers waiting on work—waste. And if the inflow is such that you have work queued up to be done and no one doing it yet, then you have work waiting on workers—also waste. We want to have this inflow and outflow happening at the same rate.

Another way to put this is that you're only as fast as your slowest operation. One subcontractor working at twice the pace of everyone else does not actually contribute to the overall productivity of the job. What you want is for the slowest operation to be fast enough, and for the fastest operation to be as close as possible to the slowest.

This brings us back to "Just in Time" delivery, and determining what you need as a constant, continuous, reliable workforce every day. We want much more tortoise than hare.

WASTE BEYOND THE JOBSITE

Lean is a better way to run a jobsite, but it goes beyond that to a broader application. This includes the construction project as a whole: There is a Lean component to everything from cradle to grave—not just the actual construction, but the concept of the project, the actual design of the project, all the logistics of getting what you need for the project, and even, possibly, the use of the project.

The thing that sticks out for me from my Lean training is the habit of looking for waste in not-so-obvious places. People tend to focus on waste of materials or time, and they see waste as related to the brick-and-mortar construction activity, but there can be just as much waste in an inefficient meeting as there is in ordering too much concrete. I have two project engineers working under me on separate jobs, so I'm trying to schedule their activities on a weekly basis so we can track how they're performing and to make sure we're maximizing the use of their time. I know there is waste there, and I'm trying to bring it to the top.

—Chris Davis, Project Manager

Also, as a company, we have administrative tasks to fulfill separate from the jobsite, and the office environment is another place where you can generate a lot of waste. A lot of wasteful office practices are just "the way things have always been done"—so here also Lean challenges conventional wisdom and ways of doing things. J. Charlie is always on the lookout for waste of this kind.

*Sometimes, in an office environment, people do things a certain way for so long, and then they teach people to do things that way, and then **they** just keep doing it, just because somebody told them to. I come across this a lot, especially with employees doing one task in multiple systems—hard copies and two different software programs, for example—which is a waste of time and effort.*

—J. Charlie Garbutt, Vice President of Marketing

We had some trouble a few years ago with our accounts payable system about checks and balances and approvals. The crux of the problem was that it was taking us a lot longer to get people paid than it should, which is not good. So, we took a Lean approach to our accounts payable process and streamlined it, took a lot of wasted motion out, and I think improved our accounts payable process considerably.

All of this, by the way, is appealing to clients and subcontractors because it trickles to them. Clients are very aware of time and money, and managers of construction affect cost best by reducing time—if we spend more time adding value, then we affect the bottom line.

As for subcontractors: I talked in chapter 4 about how sometimes Lean is met with some skepticism among the subcontractor corps, but every one of them, to a man, that we've worked with now recognizes its value, and a lot of them will evangelize for it. It's the cutting edge of productivity in the construction business, and we plan to continue to be on the forefront.

CHAPTER FIVE

BOTTOM-UP: PULL PLANNING AND THE LAST PLANNER® SYSTEM

Getting a construction job done—getting something built—is not something that just happens. It must be well-thought out. It must be planned, and it must be executed in collaboration with the folks that actually do the work. Nothing made a more significant impression on me during my college years than seeing this *not* done.

I was working a summer construction job on a dam for an Alabama company that I actually went to work for later. This project had lost its superintendent. It needed a lot of attention from the owner of the company, but it wasn't getting it, and I remember vividly how disorganized the job was, how unplanned it was, and how dysfunctional it was. I could stand in one spot and, looking to my left, see concrete block piled up with no one to lay it (work waiting on workers), while to my right another subcontractor's team was standing around with nothing to do (workers waiting on work).

For me, seeing this reinforced the lesson that if you're not organized in this industry, if you don't schedule and plan, and if you don't look after a job, it can get away from you in a hurry. Once a project gets away from you, you lose money in a hurry, and you probably won't build a good building. I told myself then that if I ever had my own company, or if I were ever a superintendent on a job, or if I were ever in charge of a project, that it would be organized, it would be planned, and it would be scheduled. I would think about not just what I was doing today, but what needed to happen every day from here on out.

This commitment to planning and scheduling stuck, and it has played a big role in the culture of Garbutt Construction since its beginning, eventually culminating in our discovery of Lean and the Last Planner System.

CHARTING THE CRITICAL PATH

We have always been a company that schedules its work, primarily through what is called a "Critical Path Method (CPM) schedule." In college, I took a course on CPM, and I immediately saw the practicality of it for any project. It gives you a schedule built on the various activities involved in a project and their relationships to one another. These relationships can get complicated—an activity may have to be finished before another activity can start. Another activity may have to be started before a second activity can start but can only be finished after the second one is finished, and so on.

A CPM schedule creates a network of all of the activities that are required to complete a project. In that network and in that web of relationships, there is a "critical path," which includes the activities that, if delayed, will delay the completion of the project. The critical path activities, in other words, have *no float*. Activities with float have a date they need to be finished by, but they may not take all the time up until that date, so the schedule is flexible as to what days the work gets done. The critical path activities do not have that flexibility.

This method forces you to first build that job in your head. You have to think through everything that must be done, and every time you think about one activity, it sparks thoughts about another activity: "Well, what have I got to finish before I start this?" or, "What supplies do I need on site to be able to do this activity?" Thinking those thoughts early on is a positive thing in itself.

So, before the job ever starts, the construction manager, whom we can call the "First Planner," has gone through a thought process about what has to be done, what the needs are, what the prerequisites for each activity are, and what the subsequent activities are that can be done once that activity is finished so that person at least has a good grasp of the project. If a CPM weren't done and all the activities were done on the fly, it would add a lot of effort, time, and money, which isn't good.

I've never tried to accomplish construction without some sort of schedule, and CPM scheduling was what I've used in my own company from day one. We still use it. It has certainly evolved and matured over the years, and it really came into its own when we combined it with Lean principles, but it has been part of company culture since the beginning.

One of my main interests in the construction process has always been in scheduling and the management of the scheduling of construction projects. This goes all the way back to my days in college and the courses I took in scheduling.

My first exposure to scheduling was back in the early 1970s, and there was no computerization of scheduling at that time. You did it all manually. I had a little brother in my college fraternity who was an electrical engineering major and a computer whiz. He got me interested in being able to computerize a schedule, so I took a course on FORTRAN—one of only two computer courses available at the time. It wasn't a required course for building construction majors at the time, but I took it anyway just because I was interested.

To graduate, I had to do a building thesis, where I took a real project—a project that had been designed and either was built or was at least a full set of working drawings to *be* built—and then did everything that was required in the administration and management of the project, from cradle to grave.

With the help of this good friend of mine, I computerized the CPM schedule, and that became part of my thesis. That wasn't required, but I thought it might help me get an A! In those days, you had to write the program on punch cards, then take the cards to the computer center and run them. Most of the time there was an error in there somewhere, so you had to redo the punch cards, take them back to computer center, run them again, and so on. After you gave the computer center your punch cards, it would be several hours before the printout was ready. Even though it was a computerized system, it took forever.

But that meant when I went into business for myself, I was not intimidated by new computer technology. When software for computerizing schedules came out, I was immediately receptive to it because I could do it on my personal computer in a matter of hours, where it would take days to run a schedule when I was in college. We've been through several programs during the life of our company, which has been another part of our maturing process.

FROM PUSH TO PULL

Once the First Planner has constructed the CPM schedule, he or she has a whole view and a good understanding of the job and what it requires. However, when that individual presents it to the folks who are actually going to be doing the work (the "Last Planners"), they glaze over—it looks like hieroglyphs to them. So this top-down plan, dictated by the First Planner, ends up not trickling down effectively to the people who actually need it, who are going to make it happen.

To address this problem in my company, we introduced short-interval scheduling, or the "three-week look-ahead." This says specifically what each individual subcontractor on the job will be doing over the course of the next three weeks. This schedule, presented on a printed Excel spreadsheet, is less overwhelming, dealing with just a small window of the overall work to be done.

The "three-week look-ahead" also allows the plan to be updated regularly. One of the things that I've learned over the years is that a schedule has to be a living and breathing document. Even though you put the schedule together and you print it out and you might put it on the wall of your job trailer, it's obsolete very quickly, usually in a matter of days—unless it's updated on a regular basis. In addition, we update the CPM schedule for a job weekly. If you don't do something like that, then it gets to be a useless tool. Both the regularly updated CPM schedule and its three-week chunks are more effective, but that form of planning is still top-down. It is what, in Lean terms, is called "push planning."

In push planning, which is the traditional method, work is pushed into production from upstream based on predetermined completion dates and regardless of whether workers are ready to start work. Push planning, then, is based on assumptions made before hand about how the work is going to go downstream—**it confuses planning with prediction.**

What Lean has taught us is that push planning is not as effective because it is top-down rather than bottom-up: The wrong person is determining what activities will take place and how long they will take. With *pull planning*, instead of the plan being "pushed" onto the workers from upstream, work is scheduled starting from the goal to be accomplished and working backward—from downstream to upstream. This way, upstream work scheduling is dependent on when downstream activities will be ready for it. In other words, work is scheduled for when it can be properly performed, not based on predetermined dates. It is also scheduled by the people who are going to be executing it. Building from the bottom-up, the team as a whole works together to define and order the various tasks into a critical path.

Push planning, then, is based on assumptions made beforehand about how the work is going to go downstream—it confuses planning with prediction.

What Lean did for me, personally, and hopefully what it's doing for the rest of our staff, is reemphasize the fact that spending time in planning actually works, and it actually makes life better for you, as an individual, and for projects as a whole.

Our clients expect us to be experts in managing trades and managing subcontractors because that's what we're paid to do. Lean, especially with pull planning, enables us to describe to them how we do it and how we do it well. Right now, it's working well. I don't understand how anyone can be a construction service provider without a systematized approach to getting everyone on the same page.

—J. Charlie Garbutt, *Vice President of Marketing*

Think back to Little's Law, which is the idea that you want your outflow of work to be as close as possible to the inflow at every level. Pull planning happens from the perspective of outflow, not inflow: what can get done on site by each trade, and when? This may slow down some of the productivity upstream, but the overall amount of work going through the system increases, which is what we want anyway. Work at every stage ends up being timed to accord with the adjacent stages, so we don't have (looking downstream) workers waiting on work or (looking upstream) work waiting on workers.

A SYSTEM THAT WORKS

The specific pull-planning method we used for the First National Bank building—and the one we still use today—is called the Last Planner System, based on the idea that it is driven by the Last Planners, the people actually doing the work, rather than the First

Planner. This is a visual, hands-on, and interactive process that was developed specifically for construction after data showed that the construction industry lagged behind other industries in how reliably it met projected outcomes on a weekly basis. As a pull plan, the Last Planner System is bottom-up and involves coordination and collaboration between the various specialists on a job, and it greatly increases the reliability and predictability of the overall workflow, so the batting average of how many of a week's tasks are completed improves.

The "Last Planner" is the crew foreman for each subcontractor. His boss can do some planning, and the project manager and superintendent can do some planning, but when it comes right down to it, he is the one who is going to execute all that planning; so, as the last planner, the guy that gets it done; he's the one that counts. Consulting with each crew foreman on how long it will take him to do each task allows the folks higher up in the process, such as the project manager and superintendent, to start building the schedule from the bottom up.

Consulting with each crew foreman on how long it will take him to do each task allows the folks higher up in the process, such as the project manager and superintendent, to start building the schedule from the bottom up.

Our first time using the Last Planner System was on the First National Bank building. The lightbulb came on for me during those first pull-planning sessions. Tracy took the idea and ran with it in weekly pull-planning sessions, and the amount of collaboration and coordination between the various trades was like nothing I had seen before in my career. For example, as I mentioned earlier, we even brought the painters in early on. Painters usually like to wait until everyone else is finished and offsite before doing their work, but we arranged it so that they could begin work on a specific floor as soon as the drywall was set. They were painting while drywall was being done on the next floor, and as soon as they finished, that next floor would be ready for them. They started two months in rather than waiting until the end, and this bought us a lot of time. The continuous workflow saved everyone time, energy, and money.

The subcontractors on Old First National really got into it. We had some who would come in fifteen minutes before the meeting to look at the board, with their sticky notes ready. I could tell they were doing their homework and coming to that meeting prepared. It was a diligence in planning I hadn't seen before.

I saw it also in the way the subcontractors all worked well with each other. We brought in the painter to do prep work on some elements in the building that we knew were going to stay before we were even finished demo-ing the rest of the building. For example, the stairwell had ornamental iron railings that were staying and that would need a lot of prep work to get new coats of paint. We scheduled so that the painter could go into the stairwell and do that prep work without interfering with the production of any of the other subcontractors. While we were demo-ing, he was prepping the iron work that we knew was staying there the whole time.

—Chris Davis, Project Manager

We did pretty much a floor a month, like dominoes, all the way up the building. One guy had to be through before the next guy got there. The whole process was Lean and worked among all the subcontractors because of the pull-planning session. In the session, everybody could see what the next person was doing. It just worked.

—Tracy Lively, Superintendent

We still do the planning on a short-interval basis—that is, we do a three-week schedule, or "look-ahead," at the beginning of every week. This is about as far ahead as we can look when it comes to getting very specific aspects of a job done reliably. Every Monday morning we have a planning session where we open a window to the next three weeks. Each individual subcontractor then commits, on a big whiteboard with a sticky note, to getting certain tasks done on certain days. The rest of the subcontractors are there to coordinate so that they all get things done in the right order and don't step on one another's toes. Each subcontractor writes a day's task on a sticky note, then sticks it on a big spreadsheet on the wall in the column corresponding to the day he plans to get it done.

At the end of that meeting, the schedule board is fixed for the week—nothing can be changed until the next week's session. During the course of the week, though, the superintendent or project manager has a Daily Huddle, a five-minute meeting in front of the board. He looks at the column that represents that day's work and says to the first subcontractor, "Here's what you said you were going to do. Are you going to be doing that? Are you on task today? And if not, why not?" And right on down the line: "Mr. Plumber, Mr. Electrician, Mr. Wall Framer, Mr. Sheet Rock Hanger, Mr. Concrete Finisher, Mr. Block Mason; is everybody in concert with what we planned for the week?" Hopefully, they are. Of course, they're not always, but then the superintendent can figure out why—not to take people to task over it, but so that the group can collaboratively help them work through it.

At the next weekly planning session, the superintendent checks in with each subcontractor about each task, asking if that task was completed. If it was, the sticky note gets pulled off the board. If not, it stays up, and the notes that are left up are the ones that have to be addressed that week. The subcontractor moves them to the day when he thinks he'll get them done that week.

As the superintendent, I've always done a three-week look-ahead. But before I started pull planning, subcontractors would just tell me what they thought I wanted to hear because I really wasn't letting them be a part of the project. I was telling them the way I wanted it done instead of them telling me how they're going to plan it. So, now they're more involved in the project, and they feel like they're part of the process of getting the work done.

For example, on a recent project, I had subcontractors working in greenhouses, and during the pull-planning session, the electrician said he was going to go ahead with his work in the greenhouses. The plumber said, "Wait a minute, I've got to get this insulated before you can do that," and they went to collaborating with each other. The mechanical piping guy saw them collaborating, and then he got in there, too. So, we all went to communicating and collaborating with each other, and we ended up with a process that told us how everything was going to come together in the greenhouses. By the time everything was said and done, everything had gone on the pull-plan board, and the work had become a process instead of a cluster.

—Tracy Lively, Superintendent

CUTTING OUT THE MIDDLEMAN

The visual, hands-on, and interactive nature of the Last Planner System makes a huge difference. You could put the same information on an Excel spreadsheet (which we still do, as well). The difference between that and then having a board that is formatted like an Excel spreadsheet makes a much bigger difference than you would imagine.

First off, the jobs everyone is committed to doing are up on a big board. Everybody is looking at that same board, and you can't wad it up and throw it in the trash can. This leads to greater accountability, which I'll talk about in the next chapter, but it also makes a major psychological difference for the subcontractor. It gives him a sense of ownership. The individual subcontractor or foreman commits to doing something on a certain day, writes it on a sticky note, and then sticks it on that board—and there's something magic about that. He's in the process then; he's not being told what to do; he's committing to what he is *going* to do, and that makes a tremendous difference.

He has made the commitment himself, as opposed to having somebody else make the commitment for him. If he gets the job done, he can pull the sticky note off the board the next week, and there is a tangible sense of accomplishment there, like checking a box or crossing something off of a to-do list. There's something really satisfying about knowing you got done what you had promised to get done.

Finally, this process isn't done in a vacuum or a silo. It's done in a very collaborative environment. When the plumber says, "I'm going to do this this day," and it conflicts with what the electrician is trying to do, then the electrician is sitting right there beside him saying, "Wait a minute! You can't do that, because I haven't done this yet," or, "You can't do that, because I'm working in that space right now." And that's

The Last Planner cuts out the construction manager as the middleman.

where the magic happens. The Last Planner cuts out the construction manager as the middleman. Previously, you'd talk to one subcontractor and he would tell you what he's going to do, and you'd talk to another subcontractor and he would tell you what he's going to do, and you had to make sure those dovetailed. In this process, they're sitting right next to each other talking directly, and that's a huge advantage. This collaborative atmosphere is one of the major advantages of Lean culture.

CHAPTER SIX

COLLABORATION AND ACCOUNTABILITY

On one of Garbutt Construction's first jobs where we were using Lean and pull planning full bore, we had a plumbing subcontractor, an older guy, who, in the early pull-planning meetings, would sit in the back, not say much, and sort of roll his eyes at the process. At the third meeting, after we got through, I just asked, "Candidly, what do you guys think about this process?" And this old plumber said, "I think it's a bunch of bullshit." I didn't like this much, but he was just putting words to an attitude I had encountered before, especially from older guys who have done things the old way for a long time. In these situations, I first point out that none of them are older than *me*; then, I just give it some time.

Over the following weeks, with this old plumber, you could see it happening: He became more involved, more engaged, more collaborative. By about halfway into the job, he had come full circle. He was very much into it, saw the value of it, and was a lead proponent of the process. He had to learn to be receptive and realize that collaboration produces better outcomes for everyone than does each party just pressing his own agenda.

GROUP SMARTS

I went through the process of learning this lesson myself—it was unavoidable as a leader. In the evolution of managing a construction company—well, probably any kind of company—at some point you are confronted with the reality that you are not the smartest guy in the room. Early on in the strategic planning process, in particular, I quickly realized that I did not have all the answers. That was the beginning of our development of a much more collaborative, communication-based culture.

Lean also teaches the fundamental truth that collaboration among people generates better decisions than does executive decision-making. The corporate wisdom of the group is so much more than any one individual's smarts. Also, the people who are actually going to do the work required are the people who have the knowledge required to make the best decisions about how to get that work done—whether it is the hands-on mechanics of construction, the management tasks of the superintendent or project manager, or the administrative tasks going on behind the scenes in operations and marketing. Business leaders need to learn how to tap into this knowledge, or they're missing the boat.

I think that we've evolved from being what I would call a dependent team and company to being an interdependent team and company. In the beginning, the company became a company because one person founded it, and that one person had most of the responsibility and passion, if you will, for making it work. Nowadays, there isn't just one person who is overall responsible for everything. We have a lot of people taking responsibility, and that's by design. Through careful planning, we've established interdependent sections of the company, and that's a good thing. I think most of our clients perceive us as team players. There's not any one thing that one person does by themselves in our company that isn't dependent on what somebody else is doing.

—J. Charlie Garbutt, Vice President of Marketing

To a large degree, the intelligence of the group is what Lean is about, and for me it is the culmination of a lifelong process of learning the importance of a collaborative, multi-perspective approach—of bringing in everybody involved and getting as many perspective and ideas about how things should be done. It has resulted in a much better decision-making process for my company.

HERDING CATS

In the introduction chapter, I described managing a construction job as requiring the ability to herd cats, and I think that is the best way to characterize the job of the manager of a construction project. When a job starts out, there could be up to fifty companies, fifty individual players, each performing different specific work on a job, with their own agenda, in their own silo. Our job is to get them on the project agenda and make them perform according to our management style.

They have to come around to that Golden Rule attitude I talked about earlier, taking off the blinders of focusing on what is best for their company and instead asking, "What's best for this project?" It takes usually three or four weeks to get everybody on the same page. Sometimes the crew comes together more quickly, but there are also often skeptics like old Mr. Plumber, but even they come around after three or four weeks. The lessons start to sink in. Getting everybody on that same page, though, is what I call herding cats.

> *I think everybody has a little different approach to how they manage their construction site. We have some guys that have a dominating personality, I guess you could say, and it takes a little bit of effort for them to open up and listen to other people's ideas and approaches about how long it's going to take them. These guys kind of get stuck in the rut of wanting to dictate that information, and that has been a little bit of a learning process.*

—Sean Moxley, President

Once everyone starts looking at the project from a holistic stand-point, the team really bonds, gels, and performs well. They eventually realize, "Hey, this is not only good for the project, this is good for me. If I collaborate with the rest of the guys and they work with us, we'll all be able to plan better, be more efficient, be more productive, and be more profitable in the long run. That makes everybody's life better, including mine." At that point, the job starts to have a rhythm where it's really clicking all the way down the line, like Little's Law says it should.

This kind of collaboration doesn't happen automatically. At this point, given that Lean is a cutting-edge development in our market, most subcontractors have not worked this way before, especially with pull planning. That means whenever we start a new project, we have a new cast of characters that have never used this process. So, there is a period of getting used to it, overcoming skepticism, and coming to trust in the process, and it starts over and over with every new project or new subcontractor brought onto an ongoing project. New players, like the painters for example, are always coming in further along in the process as the project matures, and they all have to go through the same convincing cycle of realizing, "Hey, this works. It makes life easier for me. It makes me more productive. I can trust it."

What works for me is bringing a subcontractor in a week or two before he's going to be working on the jobsite and letting him sit through the process of a pull-planning session, so, when he gets here, he isn't like a deer in headlights when I go to ask him questions. I take him under my wing a little bit before he gets here so that he has a good understanding of what I'm looking for. He has the opportunity to start scheduling his work and how he's planning on managing his guys on the project.

Recently, I invited a couple of my subcontractor owners to my pull plan, and they were blown away by it. Their foremen are the guys I pull plan with every week.

They kept hearing their foremen talk about it, and they called me and asked if they could sit in. I said, "Sure." The owners really got into it. They actually saw how we drill down with their guys as far as production. So they, as owners of companies, buy in to what we do, too. I thought that was pretty cool. It showed them how their guys were being productive on the project.

—Tracy Lively, Superintendent

When subcontractors come in early on, they tend to give themselves plenty of buffer; that is, they're going to say a task will take five days when they know it will only take three. It takes a little time before they figure out that that's not what we want. We're not looking for you to always accomplish what you say, we're looking for you to tell us what's realistic, while being a little ambitious. If you tell us its going take five days when it will only take three, then the guy that comes in behind you is going to anticipate that it's going to take five days. But it turns out he could have started on Thursday instead of waiting until the following Monday. It would be better to tell everyone it will take three days, and then, even if it takes an extra day, you're not losing as much time.

Lean and, in particular, pull planning, or the Last Planner System, work as catalysts for this kind of collaboration. Pull planning gives participants the opportunity to say "What if?" What if we did things differently? How would that affect others involved in the process? What if I didn't start in this part of the building but I started in another part of the building? How does that help or hurt you, Mr. Subcontractor? That collaboration does not happen typically unless you have this kind of planning session happening. In this pull planning environment, conflicts with the other players involved become immediately apparent.

The lightbulb project was definitely Old First National. Pull planning gives subcontractors a platform to talk about the work they're doing, to tell why they're doing something one way and why they're not doing it another way, whereas how we were doing it before, and the way I think most everybody in the industry does it, is more dictatorial. That method makes it hard to get a dialogue going. The pull-planning platform really promotes dialogue, and I've heard that from the subcontractors' mouths themselves.

—J. Charlie Garbutt, Vice President of Marketing

After just four or five weeks on Old First National, I just saw productivity take off. The communication factor between the trades is awesome. Communication is the number-one key out on the jobsite that we didn't have before.

—Tracy Lively, Superintendent

The lightbulb for me was in dealing with the electrician's manpower. He was understaffing the job, and production was slowing down. He was insisting he had enough guys and that the hold-up must be coming from somewhere else. In the past, I might have run into the same scenario but had a hard time convincing the subcontractor that he was at fault. Now, though, I could just point to the pull-planning board and show him the exact point where work was being held up, and that he needed to bring more guys in. With that visual there, I had evidence I could point to and that was crystal clear to him, too.

It was an eye-opener for both of us. Once he saw how it worked, he became more reliable and eager to schedule. He even showed his bosses the pull plan so that he could justify his request for increased manpower, and it worked. He brought more guys in, and the project just took off from there.

—Chris Davis, Project Manager

For example, the wall framer can't hang drywall until all the electrical and plumbing work inside the wall is finished. If he starts talking about starting work on one wall, the plumber or electrician might say, "Well, I've got a good bit of work to do in that wall first, but not in this other wall. If you start over there, that would turn us loose to get all the work we need done on the first wall." The wall framer says, "Sure, we'd just as soon start over there instead." These conversations happen all the time in the pull-planning sessions, and every time one does, it means an improvement in productivity on the project as a whole.

Another result is the type of continuous workflow that is very effective at eliminating waste. As I mentioned previously, we don't want subcontractors pulling off of a job for weeks because there is no work ready for them to do. Inevitably, a problem will then arise for which you need that subcontractor, and he's off working somewhere else; or, when he comes back, he has a different crew, who then have to be brought up to speed on the project.

We want a crew that's going to be there every day and that always has something productive to do. Each discipline should have the optimal crew on the job every day so that the same people are working together every day at the same pace and the same rhythm so they aren't stepping on one another's toes. That is the best way to avoid the waste of having work waiting on workers or workers waiting on work.

BUILDING TRUST

As I mentioned in Chapter 5, something magic happens when a sub-contractor or foreman sticks one of those sticky notes up on the wall for everyone to see, saying what work he's going to get to get done on a certain day. It gives a sense of ownership as well as *accountability*. They commit to doing something, and then the next week they have to tell everyone whether they got it done or not.

One of the tools that we use to keep track of that and hold people accountable is another Lean tool called Percent Planned Complete (PPC). This is basically a batting average for the actual completion of work that you have committed to: the percentage you get by dividing the number of completed weekly assignments by the total weekly promised assignments. If you told us you were going to get these ten things done, and you only did five of them, that's only half; you're only performing at 50 percent.

Industry surveys have shown that the productivity rate, or average PPC, of the construction industry as a whole is about 54 percent, which means that the production that's promised only happens about half the time. This is not very impressive, and it is here that construction lags behind other industries. Lean methods are designed to increase this average, and they do so very effectively. Our goal as a company is to do much better than this. We keep those PPC measurements on every subcontractor every week, and the goal is to have everybody above 80 percent. If somebody is below that, then we try to drill down and figure out what the problem is, and then we try to see what can be done to resolve it. Every subcontractor knows that we're going to keep that tally on him, and we're going to look at it with him every week.

At the pull-planning session, if somebody has ten things up there and he got six of them done, then the project manager writes "6/10" by his name. The project engineer, in the meantime, is capturing all of this information on a computer and combining it so we can track several pieces of interesting and valuable information: a subcontractor's performance over the course of the weeks, the average PPC of the project as a whole, and how it changes week to week, etc. Some weeks are stronger than others, but tracking PPC, as well as pull planning overall, is very effective at enhancing the overall PPC on a project.

The whole system is commitment based. From a Lean perspective, it involves what is called "should-can-will-did" planning. That is, each person that is going to do the work has to accurately depict, first, what they *should* do; then, second, whether it is practical and achievable: "*Can* we do this?" They then make the commitment that they *will* do it; and, finally, at the next meeting, they have to ask, "*Did* we actually do it? If not, why?" If they did not do the work, everyone collaboratively analyzes why it might not have gotten done. Was it under the individual's control, or was it caused by an upstream contractor not being finished with what he needed to do first, or was it caused by an external factor, such as the weather? Was there a lack of material, equipment, or personnel? This sort of question can address problems in the moment and prevent them from happening again in the future.

> If you've got one contractor who's slacking, the other guys are going to get it picked up after a week or so into the pull planning. The other guys actually pick up that guy that's struggling. They're going to be asking him what can they do to help.

—Tracy Lively, Superintendent

Accountability does not mean that we punish someone for not hitting all the goals they were aiming for. As I mentioned, we are aiming for between 80 and 100 on PPC, and in fact, if one contractor *is* hitting all of his goals, accomplishing all his goals every week, this is actually a sign of a potential problem as well. That contractor in fact is probably *not* giving as much as he probably could. He's *sandbagging*: He's lowballing his estimation of what he thinks he can get done so that he can be sure he will get it done. What we want is for his planned activity to be doable but still ambitious. Somebody always batting a thousand is not being ambitious enough. If his goals are suitably ambitious, then he probably won't hit 100 percent every week. But if he tends to hit higher than 80 percent, then he's doing pretty well. And, of course, if he's hitting below 80 percent, then we want to find out why.

The accountability aspect also leads to a broader sense of trust among all the folks on the team. As a relationship-focused company, we always want to foster trust among those we work with. Trust is, of course, central to our own relationships with partners and subcontractors, as well as among one another inside the company, but it is just as crucial between the various subcontractors on a jobsite.

From a Lean standpoint, trust is a matter of whether one trade or discipline can rely on another to get done what it says it's going to do. If one subcontractor repeatedly says he's going to get a certain job done and he never does, then the next subcontractor down the line, whom he affects, might not feel comfortable in dedicating resources, manpower, or equipment at the time that first guy says he's going to be finished: "Mr. Electrician, you tell me you're going to be out of my way every week, and you never are, so I'm not going to base my work on it. I'm going to hold back, because I know you're not going to get it done." This leads to delay and waste.

In other cases, when a subcontractor says he'll get something done, you know you can take it to the bank—that's *trust*. If he says he's going to have this done by Friday, he's going to do whatever it takes to get it done. If it means working overtime, or working Saturday so it will be ready that following Monday, everyone knows this contractor is going to do it. They're comfortable, and they trust what he's telling them, so they don't hesitate to dedicate the resources to hit the ground running that Monday morning full speed ahead.

That's the kind of trust relationship that gets developed through pull planning. The Lean approach also helps to address the problem of the unreliable subcontractor. That individual's PPC is always going to be low, much less than 80 percent. When that starts happening, one of the jobs of the pull-planning session is to have the whole team drill down to the root of the problem. Once they figure that out, they can collaboratively figure out ways to help that individual.

Only rarely is the problem a subcontractor or crew foreman who is unable or unwilling to do his job. There is more likely a different factor that can be addressed. A collaborative Lean tool that effectively gets to the root of problems is the method of asking "Why?" five times. If someone didn't accomplish one of their tasks, the first thing to ask is "Why?" However, the first answer is usually not the root of problem, so you have to press on. The problem usually can be found somewhere upstream in the process, and asking "Why?" five times should get you as far upstream as you can go. Fixing these upstream problems also has a ripple effect in addressing more problems downstream than just the one you first asked about.

COLLABORATION BEYOND THE JOBSITE

Like the elimination of waste and the importance of planning, collaboration goes beyond the jobsite. Even the owner or buyer has a role to play, especially as the decision-maker. If a crew runs into a problem on a jobsite or faces some dilemma where they're going to have to go one way or the other but can't without the owner's say-so, the owner needs to contribute to that decision-making process. We put the owner on the pull-planning board, if he'll allow us to. If he has something that needs to be addressed in that three-week window that will allow something downstream to move forward, he gets a sticky note and functions like the rest of the crew.

We typically have architects do the same thing, because they can impact the schedule, as well. So, if we can get them on the board and make them accountable, all the better.

Collaboration applies everywhere, on the jobsite and with administrative staff. It sounds counterintuitive, but I think collaboration starts with yourself. If you are not willing to accept that you're not always right, then you're not going to be able to collaborate, so I think that's where promoting the core value of being open and receptive is important.

—J. Charlie Garbutt, Vice President of Marketing

The benefit of the increase in productivity trickles right down to the client, the buyer of construction services—in both money and time. Every project serves a purpose or meets a need, and as long as it's still under construction, it is not serving that purpose or meeting that need. A store is for selling, a school is for teaching and learning—but none of these things can happen when the store or the school is still under construction. Nobody pays rent on an apartment or office space until they can live or work there. The more quickly a project can be completed, the sooner the owner or end user can use it, which is a plus for those people. Also, in so much of what we do, cost is time driven. If we save time, we save money. That's a definite advantage to whoever pays the bill.

For this reason, delivering the goods in construction service management as efficiently as possible is the ultimate goal. There are always new places to find (and cut) waste, or to improve coordination and collaboration between different trades. This is why Garbutt Construction is committed to the Lean ideal of continuous improvement.

CHAPTER SEVEN

CONTINUOUS IMPROVEMENT

Who would want their staging area next to the toilet? Well, that's exactly what this drywall contractor wanted. This may seem odd, but his story is now well known among experts in Lean construction. Let me explain. In commercial buildings, the predominant wall type is constructed of metal studs, and the drywall contractor is the one who builds these studs and hangs the drywall on them. Early in one job, the contractors were meeting to decide where each person's staging area was going to be, and this drywall contractor said he knew exactly where he wanted his staging area: right next to the Job Johnny (the portable toilet).

Everyone else was happy to let him have that spot; no one else wanted it. He had a good reason, though. His strategy was to have his crew bring studs back to their work area *every time they went to the restroom.* By doing that, he got his metal studs in place much more efficiently than he would have otherwise. He had seen waste in the back-and-forth trips everyone had to make to the Job Johnny and found a way to make productive, value-adding use of them.

That creative mind-set of spotting waste where you may not have noticed it before and figuring out ways to eliminate it is exactly what we strive for as a Lean company. There are possibilities for innovation in eliminating waste everywhere on a jobsite and in a company as a whole. That's why adopting Lean is not once-and-for-all, but a process of continuous improvement.

When I got started with my education in Lean, I had the impression, "Well, if I learn how to do this Last Planner System, I'll have this Lean thing pretty much figured out." Part of the education process, though, is finding out more and more about how much deeper it goes. It's a mind-set, and you have to continuously teach this mind-set to the people you work with. The process of looking for and eliminating waste is never-ending. You can always get better at it, and your work can always become less wasteful and more productive as a result.

I always say that, in our business, we basically do three things: We get work, we do work, and we keep score of how we did. As far as doing work and keeping score of how we did it, we are always working to adopt and develop new practices that will help us to raise the bar in productivity and quality.

DOING WORK

At the time of this writing, we have just started renovation of the Fox Theatre in Atlanta. We were selected in the summer of 2016 to oversee the historic theater's first major renovation since the 1970s. The bidding process was qualifications based, and thanks to our historical resume, our relationship with the architectural firm on the project (Lord Aeck Sargent), and our enthusiasm about the project, we beat out some stiff competition for the job.

This project presents unique difficulties unlike any others we have worked on. The footprint of the job is a postage stamp compared to other projects, and this postage stamp is on Peachtree Street. in the middle of downtown Atlanta. The theater is both high-end and historically significant, and it will still be in operation for the entire duration of the project, though we need to be finished and out of there by the upcoming Broadway season. This means that the project requires special care and planning and has become a test case of the Lean principles I have discussed in this book.

Obviously, the Fox Theatre is a fun job to get. It's one of the most well-known landmarks in Georgia. Lord Aeck Sargent recommended us, and we were one of three firms that had to go through an interviewing process to get the job. I think two things that put us ahead were our relationship with the architectural firm and the quality of our past work.

I don't know how we would have gotten it without the years of relationships that we've developed. I think the architectural firm felt very comfortable with our ability to deliver quality. I also think the owners appreciated that we were enthusiastic about the project.

For me, it is particularly special. Like a lot of kids from the area, I used to go to the Fox with my dad. Every year he would take me to The Nutcracker. It was neat for me personally to get the opportunity to meet with those folks.

Lean helped us get the job, too. We spoke in the interview process about how Lean enhances our ability to deliver a high-end product, and I think they appreciated that we had an organized process.

—J. Charlie Garbutt, Vice President of Marketing

With help from my superintendent, Tracy, and project manager, Chris, I am always on the lookout for ways to increase productivity on the jobsite. Chris is the project manager for the Fox Theatre project, and his management is entirely Lean oriented. One aspect we have to continually improve on for this project is in fine-tuning the flow of work, that rhythm of inflow and outflow at every point of the project. In particular, we aim to continuously tighten up the transferring of specific workspaces from one subcontractor to another, which could always be more efficient to some degree. As I mentioned, on Old First National, we went floor by floor, one subcontractor after another, like dominoes. With the Fox and on future projects, we are shooting to make the spaces more compact and efficient. Instead of one team on a floor at a time, we want, for example, the floor divided into four quadrants, and one team in each quadrant at a time.

Lean planning makes this possible. In the pull-planning session, all of the players collaboratively determine who needs to be in a space first, who second, and so forth. Then they work out how long it will take each of them to rough that area in (that is, install all the components without finalizing them or making the final connections), and everyone tries to calibrate these times to one another. For instance, if Mr. HVAC says he'll be in and out in three days, and Mr. Plumber comes along behind him and says he needs four, everyone works to figure out what he would need to get done in three. Does he need more manpower, for instance? In this way, we manage resource leveling as efficiently as possible, leveling time and manpower each to the optimum amount.

> The Fox Theatre job has a high cost-per-square-foot, meaning it involves a lot of work and a lot of resources for a relatively small footprint. We also have a restricted time frame—we have to be finished before the Broadway season, and even until then the theater is still in operation, so we have to have to identify operating hours and work around those, and avoid working in spaces that are occupied at a given time. These time frame constraints and the high volume of work in a small amount of space means we risk having people working on top of each other. Pull planning is crucial to preventing this. We even have sticky notes on the board representing the theater's quiet hours, so we can make sure we're moving not only on our schedule but on the owners' schedule, as well.

> **—Chris Davis, Project Manager**

If we can get everybody on that same page from the beginning, the job will soon develop the type of rhythm I have discussed in previous chapters. For the first three days, there may be no one on site other than Mr. HVAC. Then, after those three days, he moves on to his next area, and Mr. Plumber comes in. By a few weeks into the job, we'll have everyone onsite, working in rhythm, alongside but not on top of one another.

Another part of this system is that each subcontractor should leave his area just like he finds it (except for the work he accomplishes, of course). The first area is spic-and-span, clean as a whistle when Mr. HVAC arrives, so he'd better leave it that way for Mr. Plumber, and so on down the line, eliminating waste and keeping a safe and clean jobsite all along the way. This has an effect like working an assembly line—except that the workers are moving instead of the product. We have been developing this kind of continuous workflow, but we are constantly working to determine what the optimal area and time frame is to give everyone.

I see this all the time with new subcontractors being introduced to pull planning. They have to learn to think about their work in smaller chunks. I worked recently with a plumber, and it was his first time pull planning. The first couple of weeks, he would say, "I'm roughing in pipe this week." I asked how many days it would take, and he said, "Five days."

The next week, I would ask what he was doing, and he would say, "I'm still roughing in pipe; it's going to take another five days." He was roughing in pipe in multiple areas, but he only counted his work as "roughing in pipe." His PPC was shot because, according to that, he wasn't accomplishing anything week to week.

So I told him, "All right. Let's break this down to something simpler. Let's say I'm roughing in pipe on the southeast wall. How many days is that?" He said, "That's two days." "All right. Let's say I'm roughing in pipe on the northeast wall. How many days is that?" "That's two days, too." Breaking the work down into the smaller pieces made it more measurable, not to mention making it easier for the other subcontractors to know where he was working so they could work around him.

—Chris Davis, Project Manager

Lean also teaches a concept called *gemba*, which is a Japanese word meaning "the real place." The real place, from the Lean point of view, is where the work is actually happening, where the value is being produced. In construction, this basically means the jobsite. *Gemba* as a method involves those in leadership positions, planners, getting down to the grassroots level on the jobsite and getting their hands dirty.

If leaders aren't careful, their adoption of Lean will be just a matter of theory, and they'll still be removed from the day-to-day work. *Gemba* involves management walking around the jobsite, really engaging with the job and the workers at the level where they're working. If a problem comes up, the guy in charge should be there to go directly to where that problem is.

For example, sometimes on a jobsite workers run into an issue where what they're supposed to do looks good on paper, as the architect designed it, but the guy that actually has to install it discovers that the way it is planned isn't going to work. Typically, a problem like this would take fifty photos and seven e-mails back and forth between the contractor, the project manager, the designer, and sometimes the owner. If you've got those higher-up folks in the decision-making process available where that installation is taking place, though, the problem is solvable on the spot—the communication can take place immediately.

Of course, it isn't often that we have an architect or an owner onsite with us, but they all have cell phones. With today's technology, a subcontractor or project manager can take a picture on his phone and then give the architect a call right there and say, "We're standing here looking at this, here's the situation. Look at the picture and I think you can tell what we're dealing with. Can we get some direction?"

Especially if the worker has a solution but needs the owner or designer to give him the go-ahead, this instant communication can greatly increase productivity. This immediately turns the worker who encountered the problem back into a productive individual instead of someone standing, wondering what to do. Kicking the can down the road on these problems, on the other hand, can bog a job down pretty quickly. Issues that should be solvable in thirty minutes end up taking three to five days to sort out.

At Garbutt Construction, we encourage our superintendents to avoid just sitting in the job trailer—instead, we want them to adopt the mind-set of getting out there where the work is being done. That mind-set takes work, though, and is something we try to continuously improve on. The more hands-on they can get, and the more we can convince designers and owners to take that hands-on approach, the Leaner the whole construction process gets. This, as you can imagine, is also an education and acculturation process that is ongoing.

Improving our productivity and company culture, then, is something we continue to work at. Right now, we are on the cutting edge of this development in our market. However, if we sit still, resting on our laurels, we will end up being another face in the crowd. We must work to stay ahead of the curve, which requires us to continually take a measure of ourselves, see what we are doing, and figure out what we can do better.

KEEPING SCORE

Our emphasis on scorekeeping keeps us pointed toward the future. We keep score both at the level of the job and at the level of the company as a whole, always asking ourselves, "What did we do today that we can do better tomorrow?"

One of the mechanisms for keeping score, of course, is Planned Percent Complete (PPC). This is how we hold our subcontractors accountable, but it is also how we keep track of the productivity and progress of a job as a whole.

In the past, there has really been no formal way to track progress. You knew when the overall project was behind schedule, but you didn't really know where the delays were specifically. You could sense who was contributing to problems, but now, with PPC, it's pretty obvious who's creating that delay in the schedule, not only to us but to that subcontractor. If we have to get with them, to ask them for more manpower, or to talk to them about meeting the commitments that they're making, it's black and white. PPC helps us to be able to really identify where the problems are and give that information back to the subcontractors so they can use it to get better—or see an "attaboy" when they are doing well.

—Sean Moxley, President

At the level of the whole company, we focus heavily on continuous improvement at our annual strategic planning sessions. In particular, before each of these, we send out a "Start/Stop/Keep" form to everyone in the company and request that the forms be filled out in preparation for the session. Each person then has the opportunity to give us feedback on those three things:

1. Start: What are we not doing that we need to start doing?

2. Stop: What *are* we doing that is not productive or effective and we need to stop doing?

3. Keep: What we are doing that is working well and that we need to keep doing?

Every year, we have gotten valuable feedback that has helped us raise the bar in multiple areas and work through some challenges or obstacles that were holding us back.

I'm always thinking Lean, as far as what I could do to improve, or what we could do to improve as a company. Even things like staffing—could we be more Lean in how we staff jobs? I don't mean staffing fewer people, but some types of projects are better suited to certain project managers, for instance—same with superintendents. We often match project managers or superintendents with jobs based on who is available, but maybe we could be more systematic about it. Making sure the right project managers are matched with the right jobs for them will put them where they need to be and maximize their productivity, which could eliminate waste and go back to the bottom line. Are these types of processes as efficient as they could be?

—Chris Davis, Project Manager

I am currently working to systematically implement this "Start/Stop/Keep" discussion into the weekly pull planning, thus keeping score in this way on a much more regular basis. Lean actually incorporates a similar tool called Plus/Delta. The questions asked here, on a regular basis, are basically "What went right?" and "What went wrong?" The "Plus" component involves identifying what went right, and why it went right so that the habits and practices that made it possible can be kept up. The "Delta" component (named after the Greek letter often used to represent "change") requires us to identify what can be done differently, what can be done better, or what would best not be done at all. In other words, "What needs to be changed?"

My goal is to have this conversation in pull-planning sessions every week in a more rigorous and systematic way than we are currently doing. My plan, however, is to replace the "Plus/Delta" framework with "Start/Stop/Keep." This is for two reasons. First, I just think people are going to more easily and intuitively understand "Start/Stop/Keep." The words are all familiar and straightforward—I'm not sure people would know what "Plus/Delta" means.

Second, "Start/Stop/Keep" breaks things down better than "Plus/Delta." The "Keep" portion of "Start/Stop/Keep" basically matches up with the "Plus" side of "Plus/Delta," while the "Delta" side divides into "Start," for suggestions of new habits and practices, and "Stop," for concerns about what we're already doing. This gives us more specific categories to work with.

My idea, then, is to incorporate a simple flip chart at the meeting that the superintendent divides into three columns: "Start," "Stop," and "Keep." At the end of the meeting, he gives all of the individual contractors working on the project the chance to give their feedback on how the process can be improved. They can discuss anything from a conflict that has come up in the field to how the pull-planning process as a whole can be run better, for example.

Some of these conversations happen automatically in each pull-planning session, but my goal is to establish a time to reflect at the end of every session where you don't just talk about what each contractor needs to be doing on a day-to-day basis but instead step back and look at how things are going in general. Is the system working? Could it work better? All meetings tend to be dominated by certain people, and this "Start/Stop/Keep" session could also give the people who couldn't get a word in edgewise the opportunity to put their two cents in.

Over the course of this process, the operations of the project as a whole would be continuously improved. Even the project design could be improved in this way. Sometimes the folks who are doing the work of actually building and installing some of these design elements are better placed than a designer to say whether something will work or fit into the overall project. If the architect has embraced the collaborative culture of the job, then we could bring this feedback to him or her, who could then work with us on the design. In addition to the project getting constructed, then, the actual design of the project is improving during the course of the job.

LOOKING FORWARD

Continuous improvement just requires the perseverance to keep asking yourself: "What am I doing well? What could I be doing better?" Keep doing what works, and change what doesn't. This seems obvious, but the first, and sometimes most difficult, step is taking the time to sit back and reflect on those questions, as well as learning how to identify the habits and practices that aren't working for you, as opposed to those that are.

Like all these Lean lessons, this tool of seeking continuous improvement applies beyond the jobsite—although the jobsite is where I have applied Lean most in this book. I use these ideas, and this cultural shift, in running my company as a whole. We didn't realize we were doing it at the time, but we actually baked some Lean ideas, particularly the focus on collaboration and continuous improvement, into our core values.

For example, at Garbutt Construction, we celebrate doing what you say when you say—we even have a "Do What You Say When You Say" award that we give out annually to encourage our employees to keep striving to offer the best service, which is a cornerstone of continuous improvement. Our collaborative focus is part of the values of living the Golden Rule, being relationship focused, and being open and receptive.

When paired with our discovery of Lean, these values and the culture we have built around them have helped Garbutt Construction in our journey to offer the highest-quality construction services in our market and continue to help us grow and improve for the future.

CONCLUSION

During the writing of this book, I bought my wife a new car, and it got me to thinking about the Model T. It was originally made just over a century ago. Now, I had this new vehicle for my wife that, on the one hand, is essentially the same thing: a car, transportation to get you from Point A to Point B. On the other hand, though, the difference between what Ford was making during the time of the Model T and what I had just bought is amazing. The Model T didn't have seatbelts; the car I just bought has cruise control that will slow down if you're driving up too fast on another car from behind. What had to happen in that hundred-some years to get from there (the Model T) to what we have now, which looks like a different kind of thing entirely?

The history of automobile manufacturing has certainly been a story of continuous improvement and great leaps in innovation. This is not just in the product itself but also in the process of making it. The Model T was made possible by Ford's development of the moving assembly line, and it's no surprise that Lean was first developed by another automobile manufacturer: the Toyota company.

The products of construction—buildings—have gone through a similar process of evolution and development. Originally, buildings served simply to provide shade and shelter; the aim of construction was just to make the building safe and sturdy. Now, however, buildings have not just HVAC but also computer systems to control that HVAC—much more sophisticated than a thermostat.

However, the innovation in the production process itself has been less impressive in construction than it has been in automobile manufacturing. In fact, as I discussed earlier, productivity in construction has remained almost flat over the last several decades, while it has grown in almost all other sectors.

Innovation in the construction business, then, largely lies in the future, and this is the direction Garbutt Construction is heading. Our aim is to continue to be the contractor of choice for our market on the basis of our innovative practices, our being on the cutting edge of how things are done in construction. Lean is a major part of how we are going about trying to achieve this aim.

I have explored the aspects of Lean that have been particularly significant for the development of my company, but there is much more to it than even those—this is why the Leaning of a company is a process of *continuous improvement*. At its basis, though, Lean is about *eliminating waste* and *increasing productivity and quality*, and the key methods it offers for doing these things are methods of *hands-on planning and scheduling* that are catalysts for *collaboration and coordination* among the various parties working on a project. Lean involves a shift in culture and a shift in mind-set, and those shifts both require an education process that spans the entire life of a company.

That's why the story that this book tells is "our Lean journey." A journey does not necessarily bring you to a final destination where you can rest (on your laurels). This is the kind of journey that is ongoing. We will always find ways to grow and improve, and there will always be more that we can learn. I've come to realize along the way that staying true to Lean principles requires committing to continuous training and education.

My aim for the company is simply for it to continue along this journey. I am confident that it will because I have developed the culture that we currently have together with some members of a younger generation, some of whom you have heard from in this book, and they are eager to carry the company to the next level.

*Some things are always changing, but with the core values, if we continue to uphold those, we **will** always be improving. I hope we continue the kind of culture that we've developed around planning, improving, and "Lean-izing" the whole company. I've learned a lot from Dad, but I've also learned a lot from other people—our employees, customers, and partners. Construction is not a dull world. I like being challenged and challenging the company.*

—J. Charlie Garbutt, *Vice President of Marketing*

Lean construction itself is undergoing a continuous journey, particularly in our market. My superintendents and project managers tell me that our work with Lean has had a ripple effect, especially in the realm of the Georgia State Financing and Investment Commission (GSFIC), which funds and manages all state construction projects. This organization has been impressed with the work we have done for the state of Georgia—Tracy's management style, in particular—and the word is spreading that we use Lean and that it works.

I do a lot of GSFIC projects, and the guys I'm working with there are really getting into what they're seeing when they come to my pull-planning meetings. The word is spreading through GSFIC, and that organization provides a big part of the workload in the state of Georgia. I've had a couple of guys mention to me that they're amazed to see us actually doing the pull planning: "We heard Garbutt was doing this kind of stuff, but we thought that was just promotion." In the meetings, they see that we do what we say we're going to do—it's not just theory or an image we put up on a screen for marketing purposes.

—Tracy Lively, Superintendent

Feedback like this reinforces for me the value of what we have built at Garbutt Construction. In this book I hope I have been able to relate how far we have come thanks to our dedication to culture and commitment to quality. Thank you for sharing our journey.

REFERENCES

Collins, Jim, and Morten Hansen. *Great By Choice: Uncertainty, Chaos, and Luck*. New York: HarperCollins, 2011.

Collins, Jim, and Jerry Poras. *Built to Last: Successful Habits of Visionary Companies*. New York: HarperCollins Publishing, 1994.

Harnish, Verne. *Mastering the Rockefeller Habits*. Ashburn, VA: Gazelles, Inc., 2002.

Hirsh, Lou. "Businesses That Have High Failure Rates." *Chron*. http://smallbusiness.chron.com/businesses-high-failure-rates-61640.html

MORE ON LEAN CONSTRUCTION

Garbutt Construction is, and always has been, client focused. Lean greatly enhances our abilities to serve our clients.

THE PURPOSE OF LEAN DESIGN AND CONSTRUCTION:

- To increase value to the end users (customers) by eliminating waste and increasing workflow.

WHAT IS "VALUE" TO THE END USER?

- Whatever the end user thinks is most important and appreciated. This could be:
  - Earlier to market.
  - Better design.
  - Better quality.
  - Better cost.
  - Better safety & risk management.
  - Better public relations.
  - Any other values of customer.

Recent measurements by the Lean Construction Institute (LCI) have shown that Lean Projects, three out of four times, will complete ahead of schedule; and two out of three times will complete under budget.

The wastes I mention will be covered in chapter 4. These wastes pervade all phases of a project, not just construction:

- Concept.

- Project definition.

- SDs.

- DDs.

- CDs.

- Supply chain.

- Construction assembly.

- Inspections.

- Commissioning.

An owner (customer) led by a Lean practitioner such as Garbutt Construction can greatly improve all facets of his project through fostering a Lean culture, with all participants.

Efficient workflow is the second balancing point in the Lean definition. All parties have the opportunity to eliminate waste and replace those wasted resources with productive, efficient workflow.

We consider the philosophy that guides Lean Construction as follows:

- The Two Pillars of Lean:
  - Respect for the individual.
  - Continuous learning and improvement

- The Five Principles of Lean:

  - Define value to the end user, and all align behind that value.

  - Map the value stream—shortest path to that value.

  - Establish efficient workflow.

  - Utilize pull.

  - Continuous learning and improvement

- The Five Big Ideas of Lean *Sutter Health*:

  - Collaborate, really collaborate.

  - A project is a network of commitments.

  - Increase relatedness among the participants.

  - Optimize the whole, not the piece.

  - Tightly couple action with learning.

- The Efficiency Paradox:

  - Resource efficiency seeks to maximize the piece.

  - Workflow efficiency seeks maximizes the whole.

These fourteen ideas can form the culture and spirit of all of the firms and people involved in a client's Lean enterprise.

The above is the framework of Garbutt Construction's Lean Project Delivery for our clients.

OUR SERVICES

Garbutt Construction Company is here to make your project worry free and seamless. We will manage the entire job from inception to completion and into post-construction to your satisfaction. As a full-service builder, we work with owners, developers, facility managers, and design professionals daily. Our talented team delivers a complete range of professional services, including **project planning and program management, construction management, design-build, and general contracting.**

Lean Construction is a key component to our entire process, and we utilize it from the beginning of each project to elicit collaboration and unity as a team. Using the pull-planning methodology to lead our schedule, we are able to create a continuous workflow process, thereby decreasing construction time and increasing communication across all entities involved in the building or renovation process. Says Charlie Garbutt, CEO, as quoted in *Constructor Magazine*, "LEAN is a catalyst to collaboration, and a bottom-up not top-down management approach."